TRAINING TO WIN

To my loving Mum who has tirelessly supported me and my sailing career from the very beginning.

TRAINING TO WIN

Training exercises for solo boats, groups & those with a coach

Jon Emmett

First published in 2019 by Fernhurst Books Limited

The Windmill, Mill Lane, Harbury, Leamington Spa, Warwickshire. CV33 9HP. UK
Tel: +44 (0) 1926 337488 | www.fernhurstbooks.com

A catalogue record for this book is available from the British Library
ISBN 978-1-912177-21-9

The author and publisher would like to acknowledge and thank Vanhang Sailing Center in Shenzhen, China for their help with this book, providing the venue for Jon's coaching in China and taking videos and photos of it.

Designed & illustrated by Daniel Stephen
Printed in Poland by Opolgraf

JON EMMETT

GOLD MEDAL WINNING COACH & WORLD CHAMPION SAILOR

Jon Emmett is a professional sailing coach who coached Lijia Xu of China to win the gold medal in the Laser Radial Class at the London 2012 Olympics. He coached Lijia again for the 2016 Rio Olympics and has since coached sailors from the United Kingdom, Israel, Malaysia, Finland and Argentina aiming for the Olympics. He is also the Training Officer for the UK Laser Class Association.

As well as coaching, Jon is a very successful and regular competitor, with successes including:

Byte C II Class

- World Champion
- European Champion

Laser Radial Class

- Masters World Champion (3 times)
- Masters European Champion (6 times)
- UK National Champion (6 times)
- UK National Ranking Series Winner (over 10 times)
- UK Inland National Champion (over 10 times)

Jon is also author of Fernhurst Books' *Coach Yourself to Win*, *Be Your Own Sailing Coach* (ebook only), *Be Your Own Tactics Coach* (ebook only) and *Tactics Made Simple*. Jon also contributed significantly to the latest edition of Fernhurst Books' *The Laser Book*.

www.jonemmettsailing.co.uk

CONTENTS

FOREWORD

Most Olympic or America's Cup teams spend much more time training than they do racing in competitions. But the Club sailor, at the other end, tends to do no training at all – just going out and competing in their club race every week. Some countries have great training programmes for certain youth classes, but most adult and many youth classes miss out. In other countries, there are few or no formal training programmes.

It is for this vast number of sailors who have little or no training available to them, and their coaches, that Olympic gold medal winning coach, Jon Emmett has written this book: Training to Win. It covers over 50 different training exercises, each of which is classified as to whether it can be done by boats on their own, groups of boats or boats with a coach boat.

I had the fortune to race against Jon as a Youth sailor in Lasers and was always impressed by his analytical approach. It was therefore no surprise to me that he transitioned so successfully to coaching.

The book can be used by a boat training on its own, a group of boats wishing to train together, or a coach training one or more boats. Doing these exercises will, without doubt, improve your sailing and your race results. They include exercises that I have used regularly in my sailing career and ones which Jon uses with his Olympic-hopeful trainees. Masses of diagrams and photos from coaching sessions that Jon has run around the world bring it all to life and make the exercises clear, while Jon's text explains what the exercise is trying to achieve.

I wish you every success in improving your sailing through these exercises.

The person I have spent much time training with was, of course, Andrew 'Bart' Simpson. I am therefore delighted that this new book, in the Sail to Win series, is supporting the Andrew Simpson Sailing Foundation.

Iain Percy
2 x Olympic gold medallist, 1 x Olympic silver medallist, 4 x World Champion, 4 x America's Cup Challenger

CHAPTER 1

Introduction

This book is written for all sailors and coaches to help you train more effectively, be you a sailor training on your own, a group of sailors training together or a coach training one or more people.

Coaching young sailors in China

I hope that, through using the tools included here, you and / or your trainees can have the best sailing season ever and achieve your desired goals both now and in the future.

This book was written as much by necessity as by desire because, as I have worked with many coaches and sailors over the years, there are some questions that I hear over and over again: 'What is a good exercise to improve this?' 'Why do we do this exercise?' 'How do we make the exercise more / less difficult?' It made sense to put it all down in a book, so it could reach far more people than I ever could in 1:1 conversations.

Success is about focus: we need to know what our aim is and how we intend to achieve it. Therefore, contained in these pages are many exercises used by World Champions to grass-roots sailors which have been shown to be successful, but more than just the 'how' I have included the 'why' because, when everyone clearly understands the aims and objectives, both motivation and understanding are improved.

Throughout this book I have used photos and film taken when I ran a training camp for Chinese sailing coaches and their young sailors at the Vanhang Sailing Center in Longcheer, Shenzhen in China to show real examples of the exercises. Inevitably this means that they do not 'look perfect' like the diagrams, but that is the nature of sailing. Sometimes, in unstable wind conditions, sailors can be right next to each other in different wind speeds and directions and then there is also human error, where sailors are naturally early or late for the start, for example. Time and distance is a key skill and one we look at a lot in this book.

But don't be fooled by the fact that some of the photos are of children – I use all the exercises in this book with the Olympic competitors that I coach – you will see photos of some of them too! From children to Olympic gold medallists, the sailing techniques you need to perfect in training are the same!

Documenting the best way to train is so important, not just for sailing federations and training schools, but also for all sailors. This is true not only for those coming through the youth programmes, but also for the adult sailors – it is never too late to teach an old dog new tricks! Each and every one of us can improve our racing performance through good training.

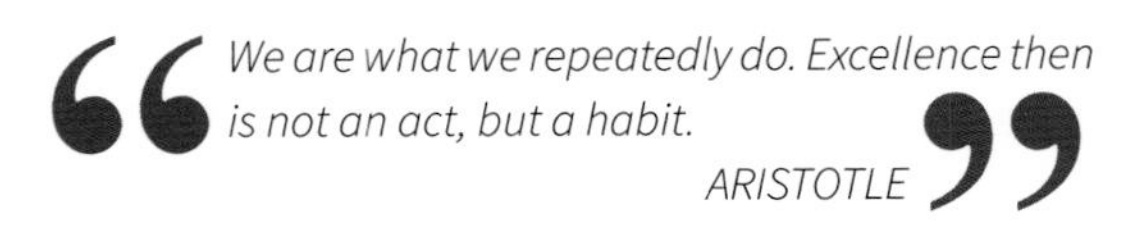

Loncheer, Shenzhen in China – a superb sailing venue

So, this book is written for sailors and coaches to get the most out of their training.

There are a number of exercises for each area because different exercises achieve different objectives. It also helps to have variety.

Some of the exercises in this book are ones which can be done by one boat on its own, many can be done by groups of boats without a coach or coach boat, while some need a coach. These are signified by the colour box the exercise appears in:

Orange Box	Solo boats, groups & those with a coach
Green Box	Groups & those with a coach
Purple Box	Those with a coach

The majority of coach-run exercises should feel 'race-like' because this means that, when the sailors experience something similar in a race, they will recognise that they have been in the situation before and feel more comfortable, whether it be having to do a sudden tack, reversing out of a situation or whatever.

Another benefit of a more race-like situation is that the sailors will be more motivated. This motivation is highlighted if the coach says they are recording the race results. Even if there are no prizes (or penalties... e.g. last place cooks the dinner), it inspires sailors to do their best.

It is certainly worth having the more race-like exercises towards the end of a session, when the motivation may be on the decline.

When You Should Train

Being in the right place at the right time for training is important, particularly because sailing is such a time intensive sport.

Looking at the big picture, you need to maximise your training time at the correct venues, which may be:

- Your home club for your Club Championship
- Where your most important regatta of the year is to be held

- Where the next Olympics is going to be

But you also need to think about the time of day to train: both making sure that you are well rested from whatever else you are doing on that day and bearing in mind the conditions where you are training. If, for example, the sea breeze is only really blowing from 12:00 to 15:00, then maybe this is the most suitable time to train and, where possible, other activities can be built around it.

Remember to look after yourself: illness and injury are the biggest causes of loss of performance. THINK! If you are feeling unwell, pushing yourself for that one extra hour on the water or in the gym is likely to negate any beneficial effect of the training. If you feel sick, over-tired or in discomfort, your body is trying to tell you something. Plan your rest days well in advance and stick to them.

A Good Warm-Up

When we undertake physical training, a good warm-up is essential to prepare the body for exercise and to reduce the risk of injury. It also improves mental focus because the mind and body are strongly linked. This is definitely true in sailing: you need to prepare both physically and mentally, especially if you have not been sailing in similar conditions recently.

Some of the top sailors may also choose to go out 10-15 minutes before the planned training session, to do just a little bit of free sailing to get comfortable with the conditions. It also ensures that they are not late for the first exercise!

If there is just one boat, good warm-up exercises (which can also be done with more than one boat) are:

Tight Circles

You don't need a buoy to do this (although it does make it easier to judge how tight your circles are): you can do it on your own without a buoy or alternatively around a RIB.

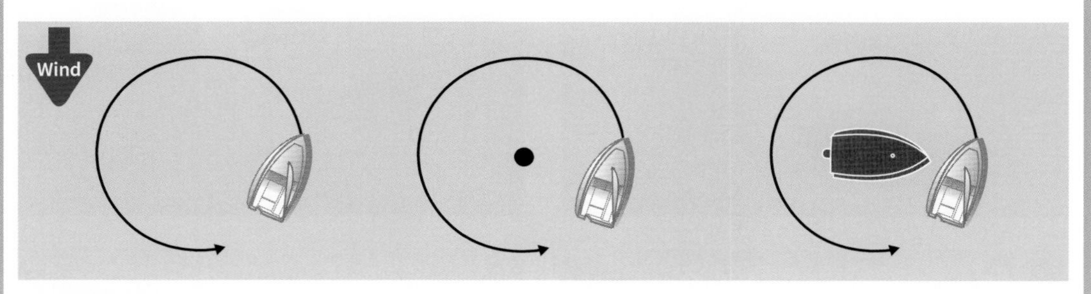

Tight circles around a buoy

Circles round a RIB

Practising 720s

A slight variation is practising 720s, but with the emphasis on keeping the speed up rather than making the circle as tight as possible.

Practising a 720° turn

Some good examples of warm-ups for groups with a coach are:

Short Course Windward / Leeward

This will help with tacks / gybes as well as windward and leeward mark rounding and laylines if the marks are fixed.

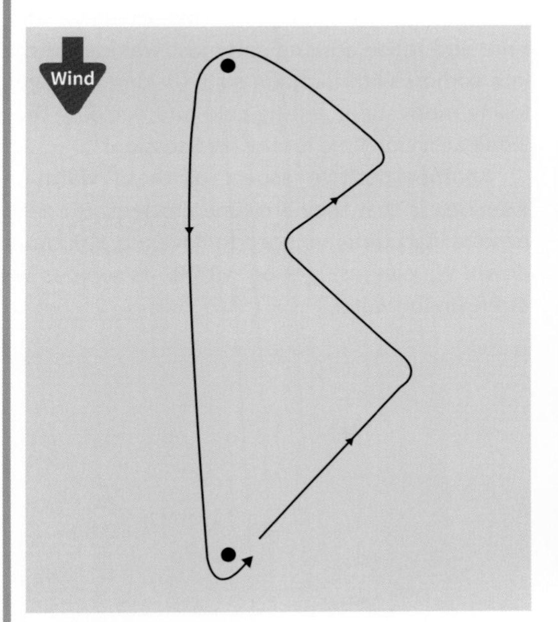

A very short course windward leeward

Short Course Figure Of Eight

A figure of 8 works well with a small group as people will meet in the middle (port and starboard); this is certainly a good way to wake people up!

This can be done either by tacking at each mark (as shown above on the right) or, to make it more difficult, by gybing at each mark.

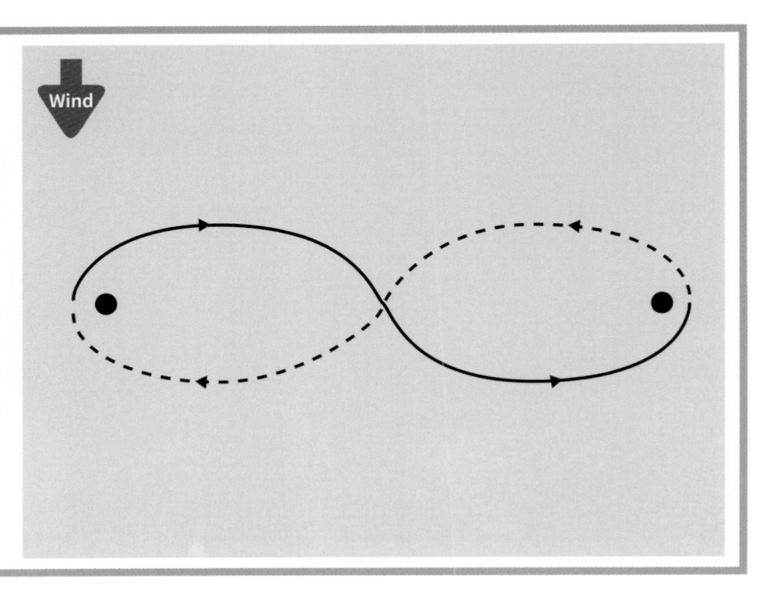

Assuming that both the marks and weights (the weight at the bottom of the mark or attached below the mark to keep it upright) are identical, the marks can just be dropped in the water, drifting equally downwind, rather than anchoring. This saves time when setting up and finishing the exercise, especially if the training area is in deep water (and therefore takes a long time to anchor the buoy).

These exercises become more difficult the smaller you make the course. So, generally, the more sailors / stronger the wind, the larger the course you need for the same level of difficulty.

Typically, 15-20 minutes on average is fine with the first people doing slightly more and people who arrive later doing slightly less.

One of the benefits of having a warm-up exercise like this is that often the group launches at different times (either because some people take longer to get ready or because there is a limit on the number of people who can launch at a time on the ramp / slipway / pontoon). Doing this sort of exercise to start with means that, as soon as some of them get to the training area, a productive session can start. This avoids wasting time and those arriving early just waiting for the late comers with flapping sails (risking damage), losing motivation, getting cold and deciding they won't arrive on time for the next session!

Another positive aspect of these warm-up exercises is that they are time efficient. No need to set a start time, no need to have a 3, 2, 1 count down. We can just 'get on with it' as soon as we arrive on the water.

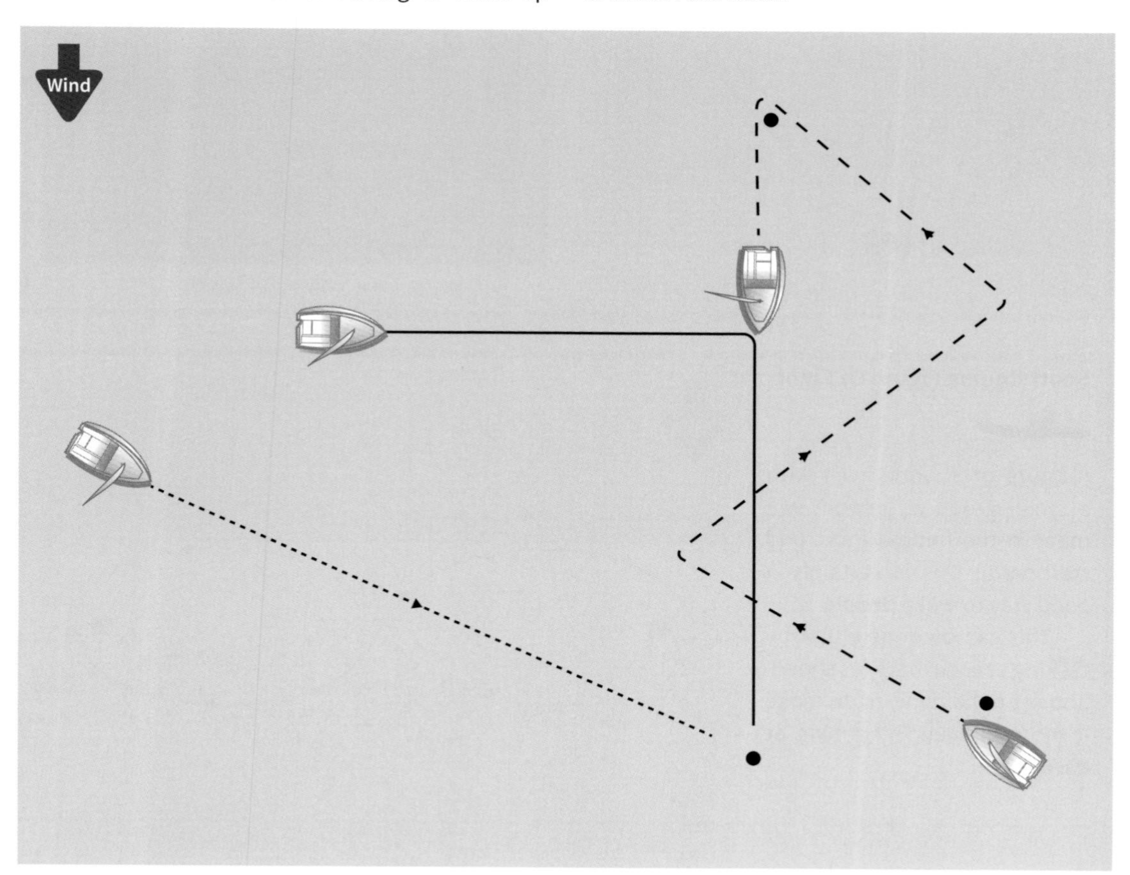

Boats launching later just join in the race exercise as soon as they arrive

Training Efficiently

As you move from the warm-up exercises to the core focus of the training session, you need to ensure that you keep working efficiently. Just sitting around waiting, with sails flapping, can risk undoing all the benefits of training. In addition to potentially damaging equipment in strong winds, it wastes the sailors' concentration and can lead to them getting too hot or too cold in extreme conditions. When cold they need to keep moving; when very hot we need to limit their time on the water. In short, it does no one any good! Sessions should be all about quality not quantity.

Follow-My-Leader

If you are going into a specific exercise and the group is spread over an area, Follow-My-Leader is a great way of rounding up the group. Here the sailors must match the speed and direction of the boat in front and the RIB can use it to gather up the group. We will be dealing with this more in later chapters.

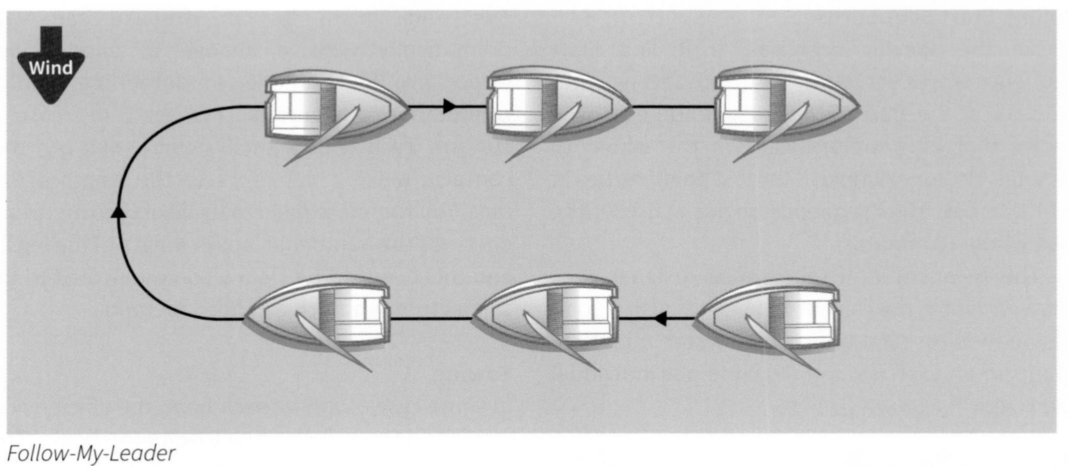

Follow-My-Leader

For Follow-My-Leader, boats must be:

- Equally spaced (the stronger the wind the greater the distance needed between the boats)
- Sailing at equal speed (try both completely stopped and full speed!)
- An equal distance upwind (otherwise one or more boats would get an advantage)

Again, people can join in Follow-My-Leader as soon as they arrive.

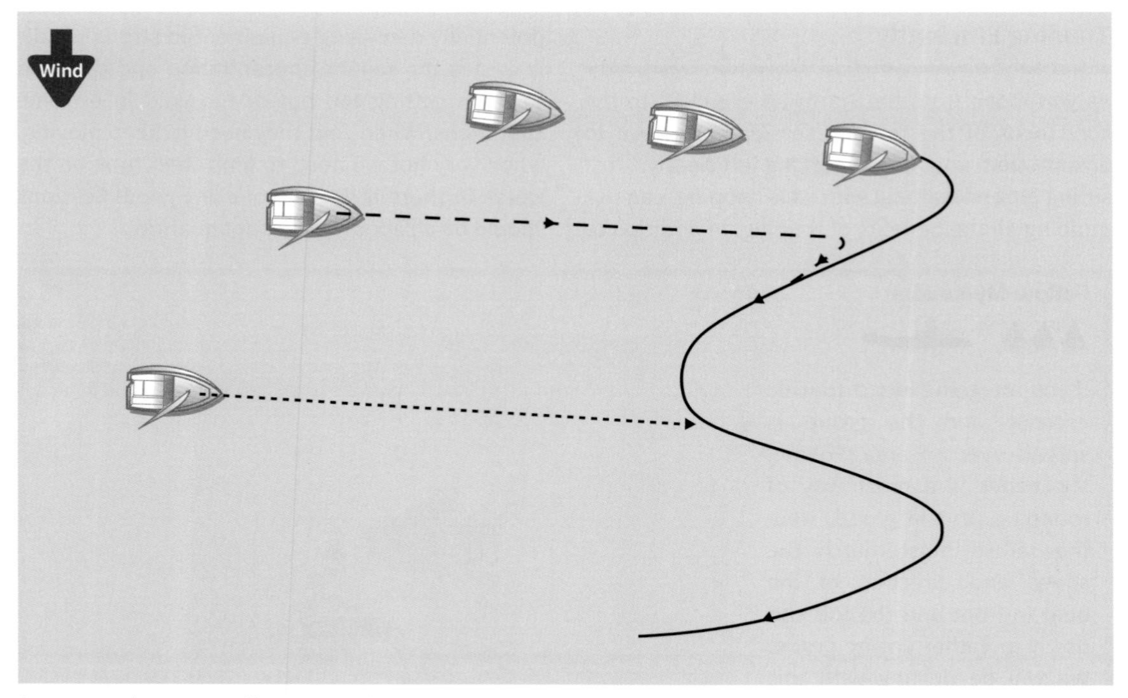

Boats can also join in Follow-My-Leader when they arrive

Rolling Start Sequences

Within the specific exercises, a Rolling Start Sequence works very well. Here you start a count-up clock at the start of the session and everyone knows that all exercises start on the whole 10 minutes. So, for example, if the last boat finishes at 9:14, the next start sequence begins at 10:00 (the next whole 10 minutes).

This means that, if sailors miss a signal, they know when the next signal will be. It is also a good way to monitor total time on the water, total time spent on an exercise and the time per individual exercise.

Time of 3 minute	Time last boat finishes
0:00	9:14
10:00	16:54
20:00	28:02
30:00	

Example Rolling Start Sequence for a training session

The time taken for an exercise can vary dramatically with a change in wind speed (especially, for example, in borderline planing conditions) or a gradual increase / decrease in current. Even with a small course, one big shift can also make a difference to the length of the race. You therefore need to be flexible to increase / decrease the number of laps or length of the legs… and this needs to be clearly communicated to the sailors through a pre-arranged method.

Towing

In some cases, with a coach boat, the efficiency of the session is improved by towing the boats. This might be out to the area to begin with, back at the end of the day or to allow the focus to be just on downwind work (towing them upwind) or upwind work (towing them downwind).

Having towed hundreds of sailors in this way, there are a few points worth noting:

- The longer the length of the tow rope the better: it provides a more comfortable ride for the sailors, but be careful someone doesn't try to sail between you and the sailor and over the tow line!

- The towed boats need to be away from the "V" of water behind the RIB and in the flat dead water zone.
- If you have 2 lines of boats behind, try to have the length of tow ropes very slightly different, so the boats are not side-to-side to avoid being bumped if someone loses concentration.
- Make sure that the tow rope is attached to a strong point on both the RIB and the boats being towed. In a perfect world the tow ropes go through each other rather than loading the boat (2 bowlines around the mast for example).

Towing upwind

If you are towing a number of boats downwind (e.g. to concentrate on upwind work):

- Make sure that everyone is lined up with their sails flapping before heading off downwind: you don't want to collect people for a tow going downwind.
- To make the tow worthwhile (and actually save time rather than the boats sailing downwind themselves) you will need to be towing relatively fast and the sails will come into the centre of the boat and crew weight can therefore be centred.
- It may even be worth taking sails down if it is easy to do this in the particular class.

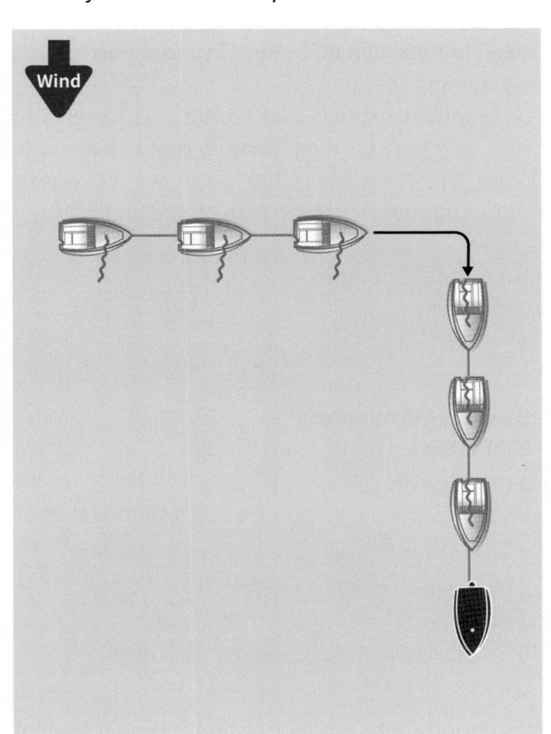

Towing downwind (to do an upwind session)

How To Finish

It is often worth finishing a training session on a 'normal' race before the first day of a regatta, so the sailors go on the water the next day in fleet racing mode.

CHAPTER 2

Starting

Increasing The Number Of Practice Starts

The start is the time in a race when it is possible to gain or lose the most places. It therefore stands to reason that this is a key area to practise. With club racing you may be able to practise 1 or 2 starts a week, but you can do 3 starts in a 9-minute period in a training session.

Experience shows that a ratio of 3:1 seems to work very well for most people, that is 3 starts to 1 race on a 9-minute rolling sequence. So, a start every 3 minutes and then race on the final start:

3 minutes (9 minutes) 2 minutes 1 minute 0	 Go – 1st practice start
3 minutes (6 minutes) 2 minutes 1 minute 0	 Go – 2nd practice start
3 minutes (3 minutes) 2 minutes 1 minute 0	 Go – 'real' race

It is important to appreciate that it is only evident about 30 seconds after the start whether you have got a good start or not. For example, you could have been slightly behind the line but with very good speed and had a great start, or you could have been bang on the line but with poor speed and had a very bad start.

You need to continue for at least half a minute after the starting signal to see how advanced you are to windward and if you have a clear lane (i.e. you can sail in clean wind at a good close-hauled angle) to where you want to go (with no boats slowing you down).

The length of the 'real' race (short, medium, long) and type (Short Course Windward / Leeward, Gut Buster, Upwind Riverboat etc.) depends on what other objectives you have set for the day. Alternatively, you may have been working as a small group of around a dozen boats (maximum) on boatspeed and then everyone comes together for practice starts and races at the end of the session / day.

The Elements Of Good Starting

Acceleration

Acceleration out of the start is incredibly important. Your position and timing can be perfect but, if you cannot accelerate fast enough, you will not have a good start. It is tempting to believe that

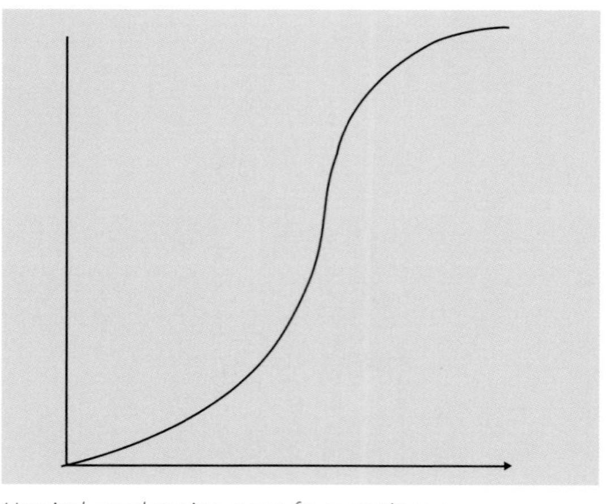

Upwind acceleration curve from stationary

you can just start to accelerate early but, if you start to accelerate earlier than the boats around you and they have better acceleration, then they will pass you.

Just like a car, it takes time for a boat to accelerate to full speed and it is much harder for it to accelerate from completely stopped than from a 'rolling start'. This is because when there is water moving over the foils, they grip better. Indeed, you can see some classes of boat slip very slightly sideways if they sheet in from stopped on a close-hauled course.

It can take some time to get that final 10% of boatspeed and the difference between 90% and 100% full speed can be very hard to detect (because they feel almost the same).

Hitting The Line At Full Speed

A very good exercise is to work out at which point you are at full speed. Set up a line and, rather than sitting on the line, sit a long way back and then, with less than 1 minute to go, go full speed and aim to be on (not over or behind!) the line at the start. You may be surprised at just how long it can take to get up to full speed (as opposed to 90%). If in a group, you can shout or wave a hand: a) when at full speed, b) when crossing the line.

It is especially important to do this exercise around race time or in similar conditions to those you will be racing in, because the conditions will affect how long it takes you to get up to full speed.

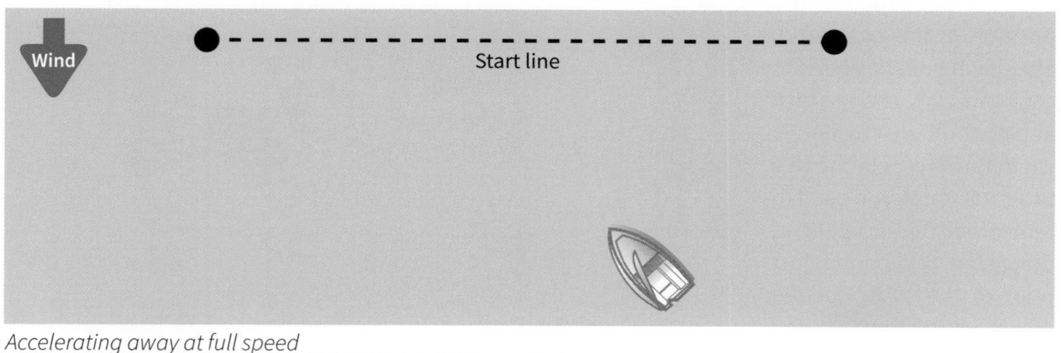

Accelerating away at full speed

Some sailors choose to turn off their ratchet blocks at the start to make them silent so that the other sailors cannot hear them beginning to accelerate but, all things being equal, the best option is to go with your own timing and a good acceleration.

For acceleration you need space to windward, so you cross the line at full speed, but also space to leeward, so that you can bear away to a point where the boat accelerates quicker. A reach is a faster point of sailing than close-hauled and a boat will accelerate much faster on a reach than close-hauled. Indeed, a boat above a close-hauled course will accelerate very slowly.

TOP TIP

As an aside, this is also the angle that you should initially exit a tack at. The leeward heel then allows the boat to head up to the close-hauled course where the boat is balanced (by being rolled flat) to encourage it to continue in a straight line as well as bring it up to full speed.

Trigger Pulls

The best practice for acceleration needs no line, just 3 boats lined up, completely stationary (because it is harder to accelerate from being stopped), close-hauled.

The middle boat gives a countdown: "3, 2, 1, go". After a few boat lengths it will be obvious one boat is ahead and then you can stop the exercise and reset. You should rotate the position of the boats and, after each boat has been in each position, change tack and go through it again.

In terms of relating this to actual starts, you need to remember this is, in effect, practising the period just prior to the start, not the actual start time – you need to have accelerated before the start.

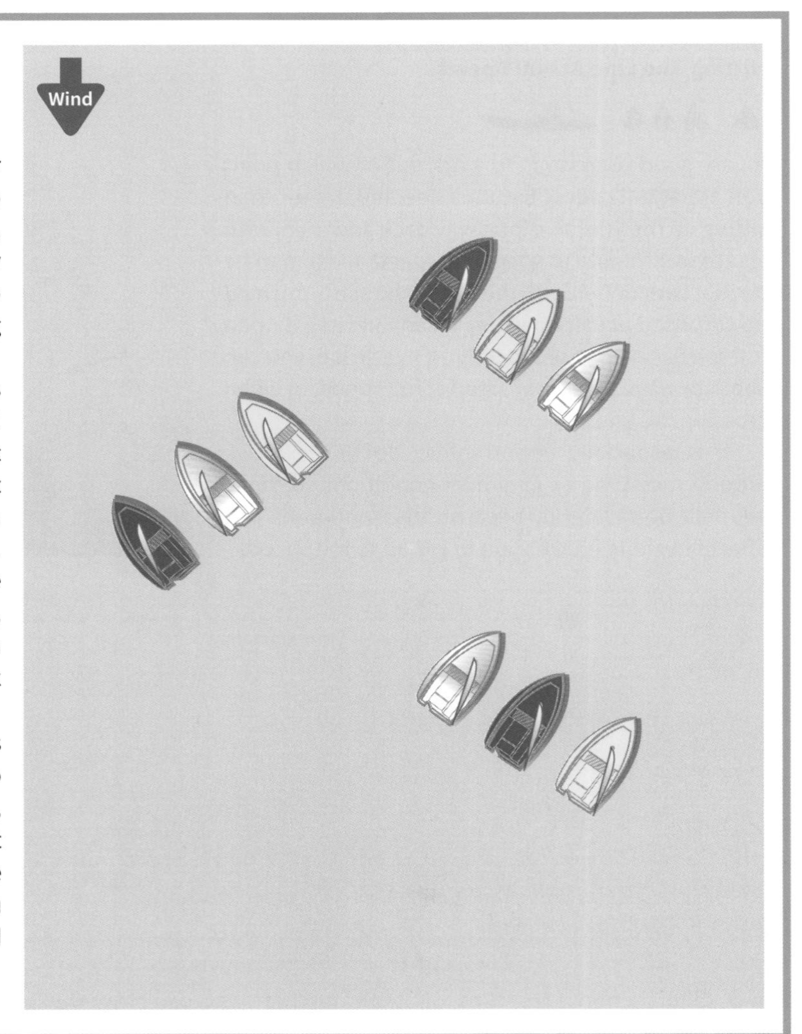

Positioning

As well as having great acceleration you need to be in the right position.

Firstly, knowing when you are on the line is key and this is especially hard in the middle of a long line.

Mid-Line Stop

Practise stopping (not going forwards OR backwards) completely just behind the line, right in the middle, raising your hand when you are there. It is not as easy as it sounds.

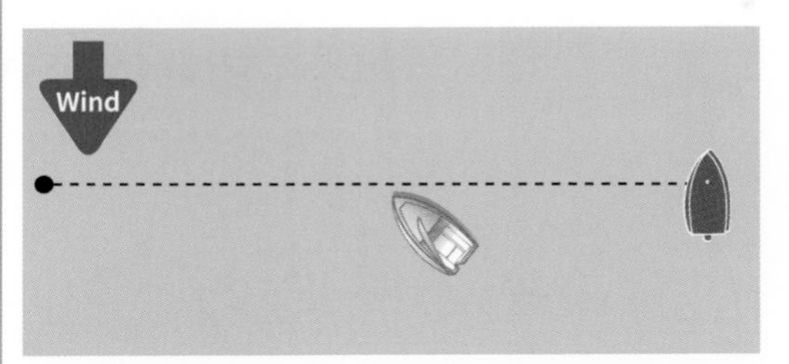

Try sailing to the middle of the line

And raise your hand when you are there

Normally there will be some bias on the start line, with either the start boat or pin end mark more upwind than the other (although this may vary with a constantly changing wind direction). If there is a bias, you will usually want to start further upwind than your rivals.

TOP TIP

If the start line also acts as a downwind gate, and the wind direction remains unchanged, then the favoured end of the start line (most upwind) will also be the favoured end of the leeward gate to round. On a very biased line, the other mark is unlikely to get a look in.

However, you may want to start at one end for strategic reasons: it is easier to go left if you start by the pin and easier to go right if you start by the committee boat.

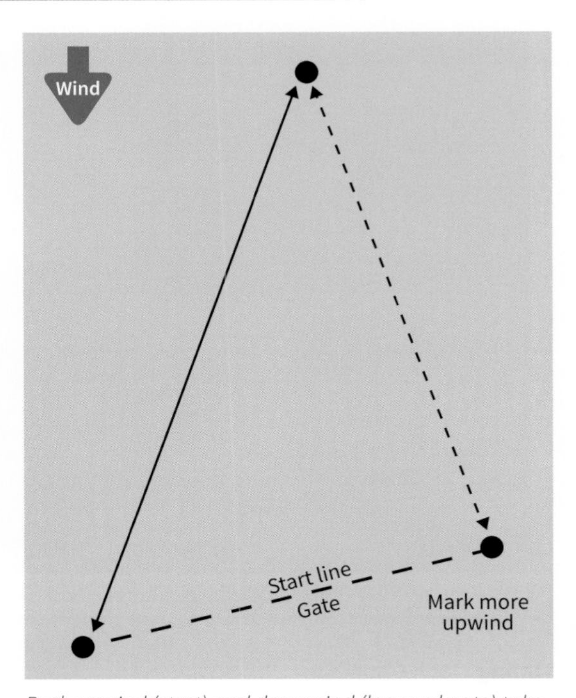

Both upwind (start) and downwind (leeward gate) take the mark further upwind

Winning The End

It doesn't matter whether your actual start would be influenced more by line bias or strategic considerations, the point of this exercise is to win the end (i.e. be the closest boat to your chosen buoy). So, even if the line is port biased, the aim when starting at the starboard end of the line is to start as close to the starboard end as possible (so you could tack and be the first boat to the right).

A good way of doing this is dividing into odd and even sail numbers or, better still, have bibs (black and white or whatever) so half the fleet starts at one end and half the fleet starts at the other end. You could even have a RIB in the middle of the line, separating the 2 groups.

This exercise is all about positioning and the aim, within each group, is to be right by (but not touching) the mark at the 'start' which we get to with a 3-minute countdown.

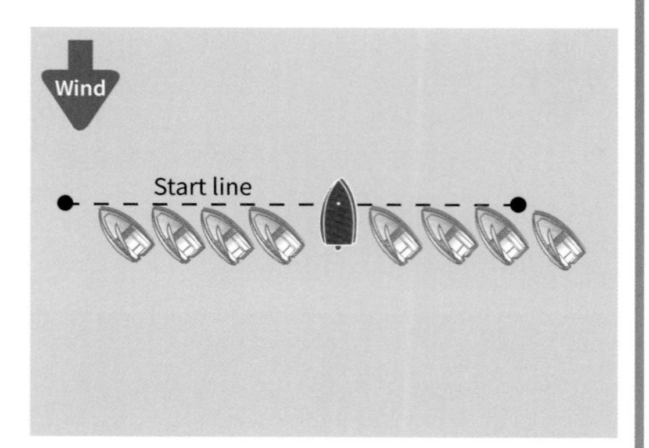

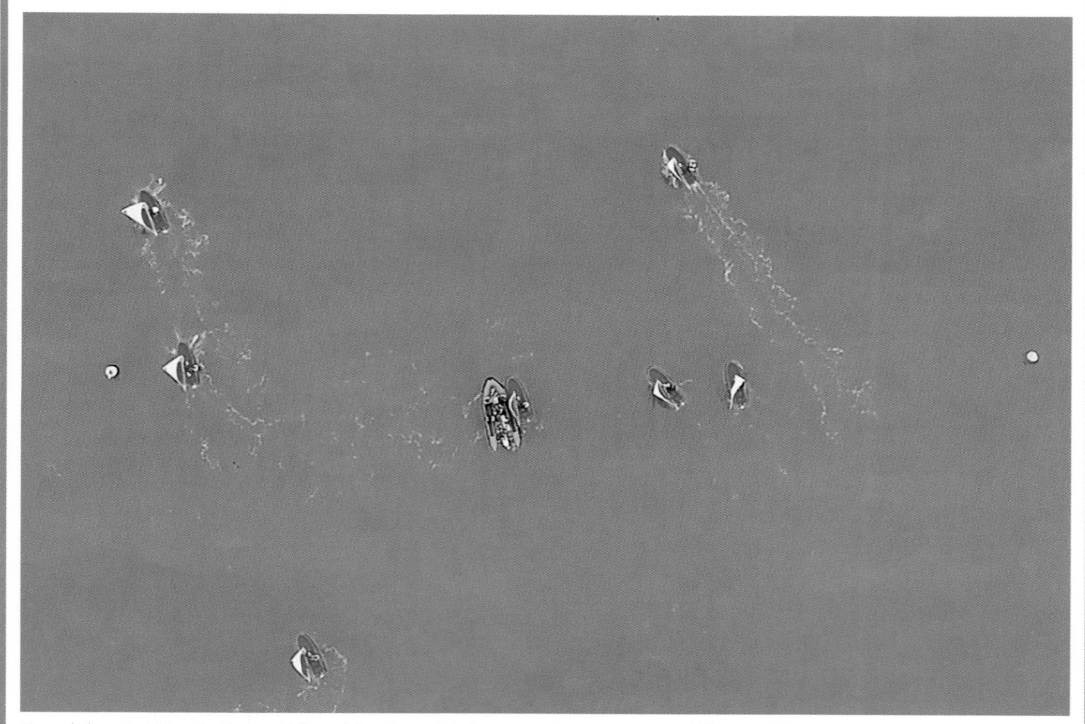

Coach boat sitting in the middle of the line with boats trying to start in different places

Timing

But, of course, starting isn't just about positioning, it is also about timing: we need to be able to line up in position and hold that position until it is time to accelerate.

Variable Start Time

So, in this exercise we have a variable start time. We have the 3-minute, 2-minute, 1-minute sequence, but the 'go' could be 30 seconds early or 30 seconds late. This encourages the whole fleet to line up early and hold position.

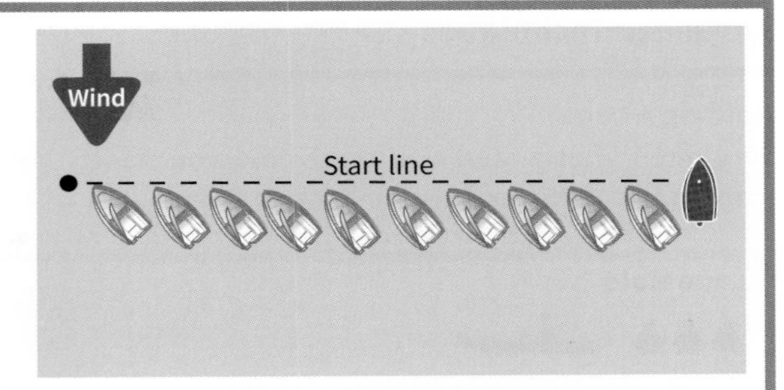

Boats holding position, waiting for the 'go'

In regattas, the higher the quality of the fleet, the earlier they tend to line up – it's just like getting a car parking space at the cinema: the earlier you arrive before the first film, the better your chance of getting a good car parking space!

Favoured End

Finally, we could have a more 'free' start / race. Here the line can be repeatedly changed (maybe while the sailors are doing a short race) so that the favoured end may or may not change every start. This means that the sailors need to check the line bias frequently (which is, after all, a very good habit).

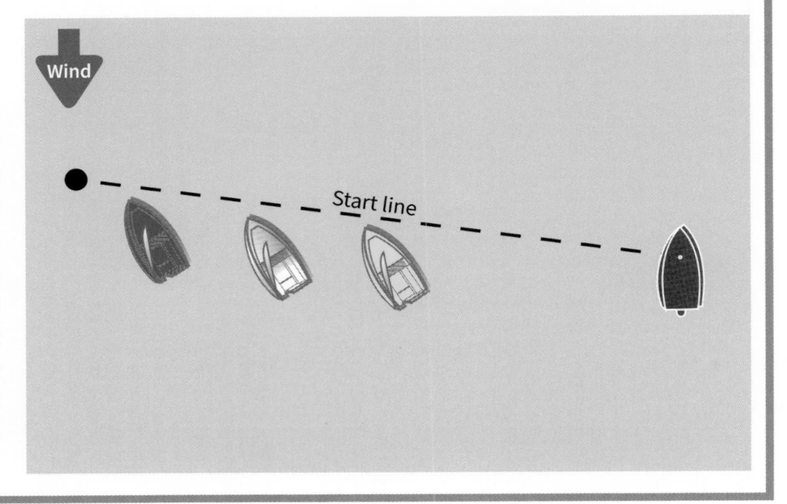

As always, these exercises may or may not progress into races. If in doubt, 1 race in 3 starts, as mentioned earlier, works well: go into a race on the third start.

Advanced Techniques

Holding A Lane

Very often after a start you must hold your lane (continuing on your existing tack at good VMG without being affected by the boats around you through dirty air / leebow effect etc.) because otherwise you will get bad air or have to sail a lot of extra distance:

- If you try to go low, then you may end up being

Lane Hold

The perfect exercise for this is the Lane Hold: there is a standard 3,2,1, go sequence, but the aim is to get upwind on one tack to level with a buoy, perhaps a 3-minute sail upwind.

Of course, in a real race, after a poor start a boat may be able to get out of the dirty air / leebow effect by footing off (losing some ground to windward but better than sailing in dirty air) or tacking off (again getting into clear air). But the point of this exercise is to learn when you can hold a clear lane and when you can't. The narrower the lane you can hold the better, so pushing it to the limit in training will help you understand this.

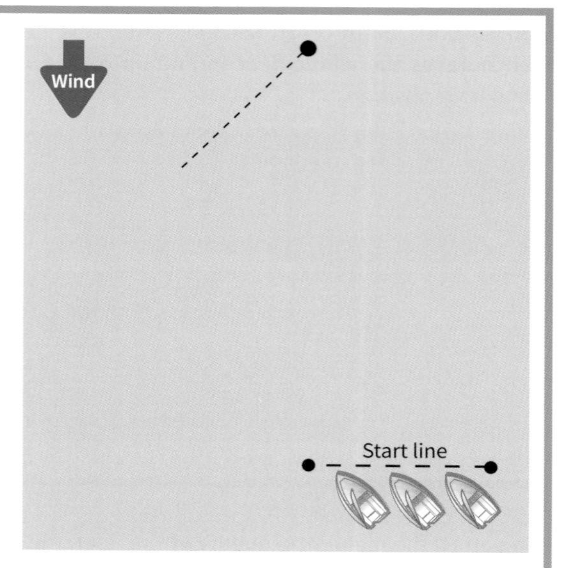

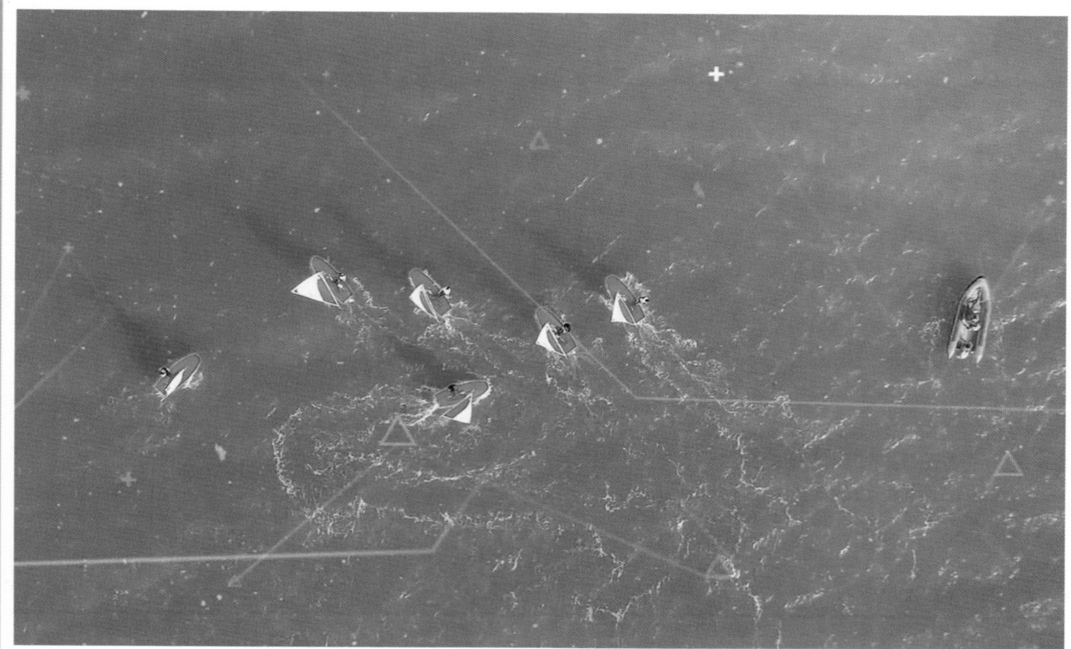

After the start, try to hold your lane for 3 minutes

leebowed by the boat to leeward
- If you try to pinch, someone to windward is likely to roll you and give you dirty air as well
- If you tack you may have to duck many boats and sail a greater distance

In these scenarios it is best to keep going (as fast as you can!) until an opportunity presents itself to do something different.

So, being able to hold your lane is very important. The higher the level of competition the more important this becomes.

Often you may have to hold your lane with other boats in very close proximity, either because you definitely want to go one way (for example, if there is an expected shift or there is better current) or because you are not in a position to tack without having to duck a lot of boats and thereby lose a lot of places.

Rabbit Start

It is not always possible to have starting marks or, indeed, someone to monitor the line. A Rabbit Start is a great way of starting an exercise and it also practises your ability to judge speed and distance.

Rabbit Start

The 'Rabbit' sails across the fleet on a close-hauled course (very important they don't reach in at speed as everyone has to be able to judge their approach). Boats then cross at full speed, on a close-hauled course behind the Rabbit.

When everyone has passed behind the Rabbit, the Rabbit tacks (maybe 2 boats past the last boat, but this is wind strength and boat class dependent).

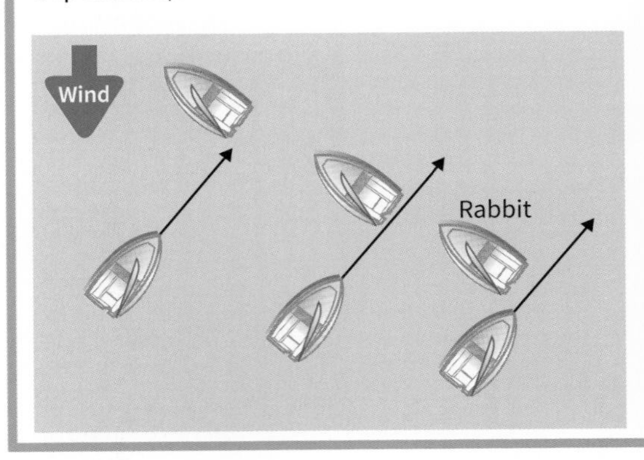

Rabbit Start

Controlling The Boat

The most important thing is controlling the boat. The advanced exercises overleaf will really push some of you to practise on your own, others in groups. These are time and distance / boat handling exercises. Remember that, even though you will typically be lining up on starboard tack on a start line, you should also practise on port tack because these are incredibly useful boat handling exercises in their own right.

There are individual exercises and group exercises shown overleaf.

Kiss The Buoy

Line up by the buoy with the bow just off it. Accelerate and sail upwind. Tack and reach off, gybe round and then up under the buoy, stopping with the bow just touching (kissing) the buoy and repeat.

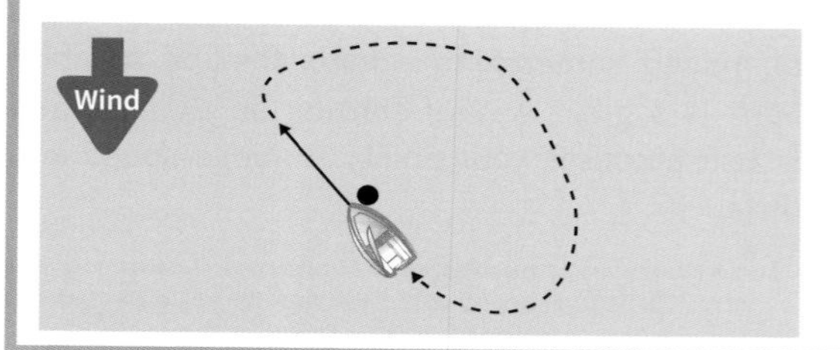

Line up with the bow just off the buoy

Around The Buoy In One Tack

Line up by the buoy with the bow just off it. Accelerate and sail upwind. Go head to wind and then back the sail. Reverse past the buoy (remember the rudder is also working in reverse) and then line up under the buoy, touching it ever so gently again (kissing it!).

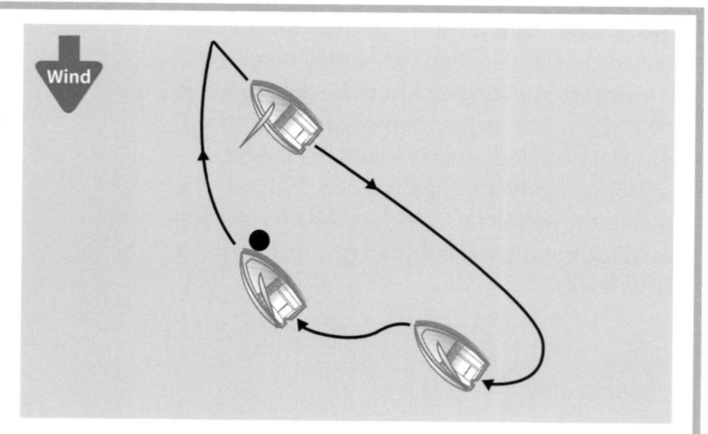

Reverse past the buoy

Move Up The Line, Reversing Out

To continue practising the reverse out, but in a group exercise, line up near the port end of the line. The most leeward boat then reverses out, tacks and then tacks again to take up the windward position. The new leeward boat repeats this and so on.

The most leeward boat reverses out

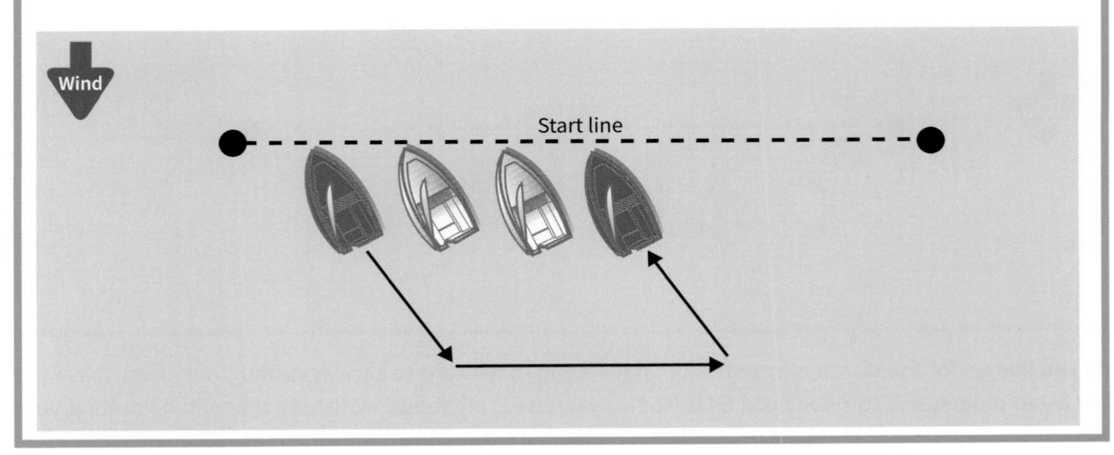

Move Down The Line, Reversing Out

Once you are all the way up the line and the windward boat can no longer cross the line, reverse the process. The most windward boat reverses out, bears away and then moves to the leeward position. The new windward boat repeats this and so on until you've gone all the way down the line.

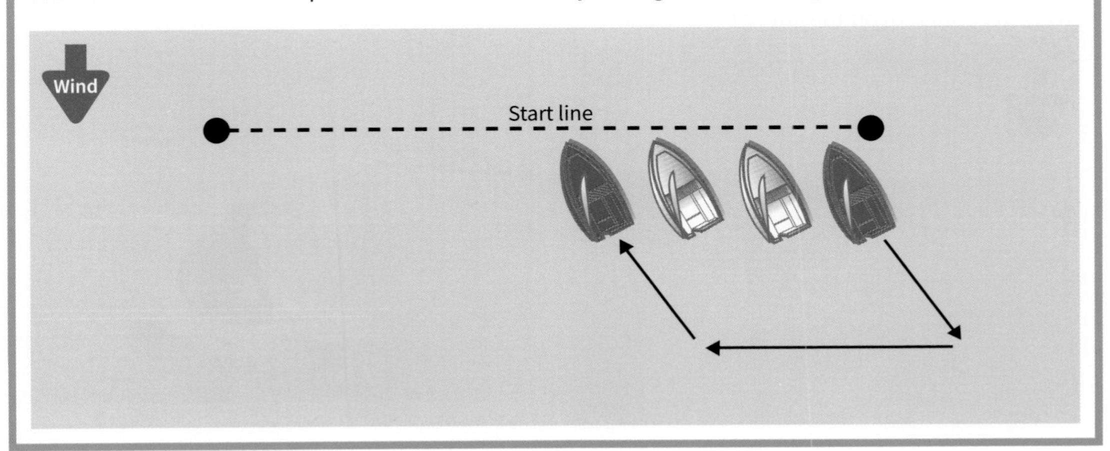

Double Tacking Up The Line

Having moved up and down the line, it is time to go back up again! This time the windward boat creates more leeward space by doing 2 quick tacks without going over the line. As soon as it is lined up again, then the next boat does a double tack and so on.

Double tacking on the line

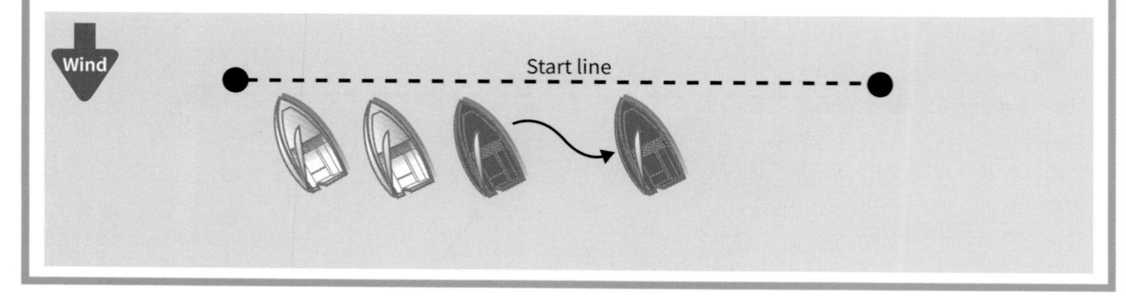

As you line up for the start it is important to have a gap to leeward to accelerate into. But, if you leave too big a gap to leeward, someone will fill it, so this exercise is all about protecting that gap by putting your bow down into the gap. If you have your bow down before someone has an overlap, if they then force you up, you will still have a gap.

Guarding The Gap

Come up to the line (near the middle), sheet in, head up to head to wind and then put the bow down, rather than simply drift down the line. Having held this position for a while, luff up and then bear away to accelerate off the line, as if for a start.

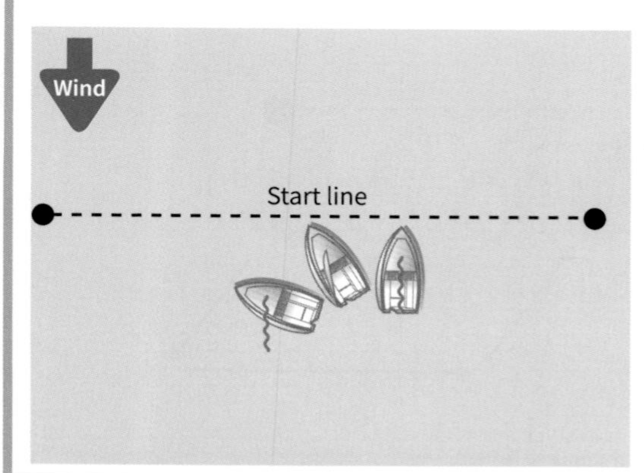

Bear away to guard the gap

CHAPTER 3
Tacking

Light Wind Tacking

Light wind tacking is all about being physical with the boat, so that the battens pop in a fully battened main or the blocks travel cleanly to the other side of the traveller, for example, in the Laser.

The more of our energy we can put into the boat the better, so the order of priority is:

- Body roll to turn the boat
- Pumping the sheet to come out on a new close-hauled course with the correct set up
- Steering

When tacking with a fully battened sail, the battens need to 'pop'

Laser traveller blocks need to travel cleanly across

For example, if we do not roll the boat enough, we can correct this with a forceful pump of the mainsheet. The last option is the rudder as this can slow the boat down.

The roll happens at the head-to-wind point. In light winds, too little roll is much worse than too much roll so, if we have insufficient roll, we can pull the boat on top of us as we move to the other side.

Pulling the boat on top of you using your back hand to increase the roll while still facing forward

The feel of the boat as you exit a tack should be that it wants to accelerate back to full speed on its new close-hauled course rather than wanting to continue to head up (which it would do if there were too much leeward heel) or bear away (if there were too much windward heel).

Strong Wind Tacking

As the wind gets stronger, there is generally a gradual transition between techniques although in some classes there may be a sudden change at a certain wind speed. However, in most cases, we simply gradually reduce the amount of roll as the wind speed increases, until in strong winds we keep the boat more or less dead flat and in survival conditions the key is to move across the boat as fast as you can. (These transition points vary from class to class.)

When racing, the conditions may well change during the race, which means you need to 'change gear' not only for the boat set-up and sailing style to maximise boatspeed, but also for boat-handling manoeuvres. It therefore pays both to get an accurate weather forecast and to 'keep your head out of the boat' to spot any changes.

Tacking Exercises

Simply setting a short course for the wind strength will increase the frequency of tacks but often we will wish to do specific exercises:

Tacking On The Whistle

The name is key here: it is Tacking On The Whistle, not tacking when you want (either early or late). This forces you to tack when you may not wish to in terms of a header / gust / lull etc.

In terms of analysis this is very easy: since everyone tacks at the same time, it is easy to judge who has the best technique in the group and, if you have someone in a RIB blowing the whistle, then they can easily video as well. Now with 4K video readily available you can easily see a lot of detail.

To increase the difficulty, blow the whistle more frequently or progress into double, triple or an even greater number of tacks (where you blow the whistle as soon as the previous tack has been completed). The importance of making it more difficult is that it highlights weaknesses, especially in multi-crewed boats when the sailors are put under time pressure.

Key points:

1. It is Tacking On The Whistle, not before, after or when you feel like it.
2. Everyone must start equally (3 options):
   A. Start Line: You can start Tacking On The Whistle from a normal start line. This is a good option if your group needs more starting practice.
   B. Rabbit Start: Good if linking with a

boatspeed session or for large groups (where it may be difficult to do a start line without some boats being over the line and the need to recall).

C. Follow-My-Leader: A great way to start the first session as you can use the Follow-My-Leader to gather up the whole group after launching.*

* See p17 for more details about Follow-My-Leader.

Upwind Riverboat

This exercise requires 3 RIBs. The first of these acts as a windward mark, the next two as a start line.

Once the race has started the sailors need to keep in the triangle formed by all three boats. As the boats progress upwind the triangle gets smaller and they have to tack more.

Start with the usual 3-minute sequence. Normal racing rules apply, and sailors can call water for the 'river bank'. Coaches may need to whistle to indicate when sailors are over the 'river line'.

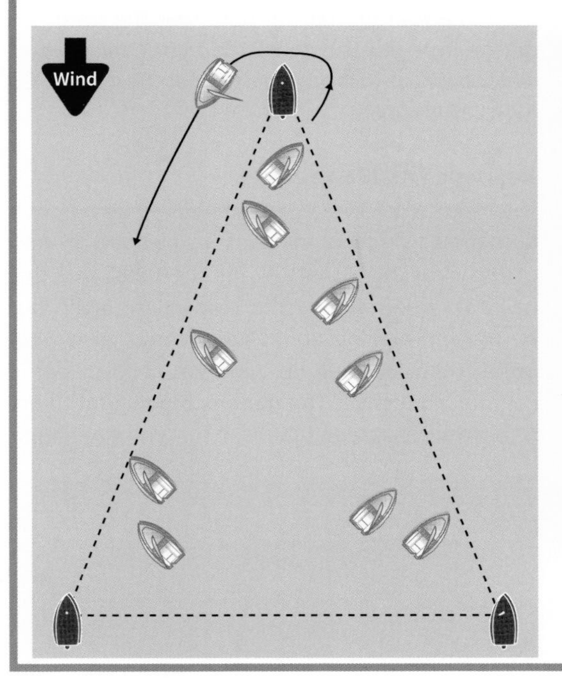

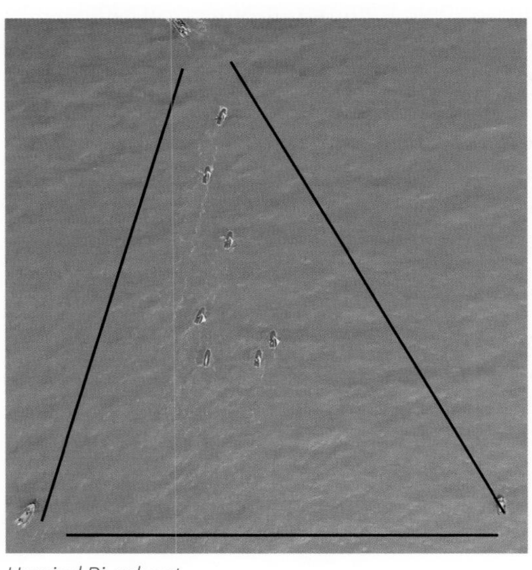

Upwind Riverboat

Progression: The RIBS can go slowly upwind too, meaning that the more competent sailors end up at the top of the triangle doing lots of tacks, whereas the weaker sailors are further back, tacking less.

Further progression: Those sailors who get to the top mark may round and go back to the start. This then becomes great practice for pulling through the fleet. This exercise can also be used to progress the training group to an upwind racing course or can be a good motivator at the end of a session (when they round the top mark they can go home!).

However, in strong winds you may consider doing this exercise when sailors are at their most fresh as the possibility of boat-to-boat incidents could increase with fatigued sailors: so, consider what time of day is best to do this exercise.

CHAPTER 4

Gybing

Choosing The Gybe For The Conditions

Although the hand and feet movements may seem very similar when tacking and gybing, the end goal is very different: in fact, it is the opposite. When gybing from run to run, we are looking to maximise our gain made downwind. That is our focus: not how fast we can come out of the turn but, 20 seconds after the gybe: how much progress we have made downwind? In recent years with the increased use of drone footage we have been able to see this really clearly. Practice is very important here: try different angles, in different wind speeds and see what works best.

Spinnaker work is all about talking, good communication, where and when are you going to gybe. So, unlike a one-sail boat where you may just exit the gybe on the new desired course, you may initially need to go slightly high to help fill the spinnaker which will then generate apparent wind, allowing you to bear away. Alternatively, you might need to keep low, until all the crew are safely across to the new windward side of the boat, before heading up.

It is also important to note that the faster we are on entry to the gybe, the better the flow of water over the foils and so the safer the gybe is. Go for it… full speed!

Respect The Manoeuvre

Sometimes there is more of an element of fear of the gybe than there is for the tack, and this helps no one. We need to respect the gybe but be brave. Thinking about what could go wrong, rather than focusing on what we need to do, is counterproductive. The mind is a powerful thing. If someone says 'don't think about pink elephants',

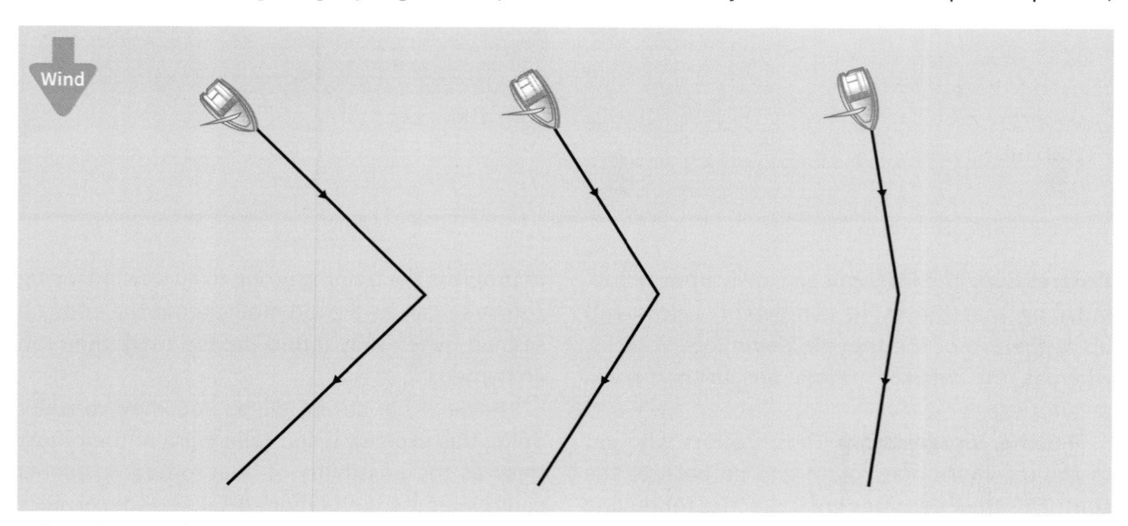

Gybing downwind: Speed or distance, which is better?

it is very hard not to think about pink elephants... in other words we don't really process negatives. So, the focus always needs to be on something positive, like moving across the boat quickly and smoothly (not like a pink elephant!).

Few people have the same concerns about tacking. After all, if you do capsize, it is normally a slower thing and often to leeward and it can usually be saved easily by simply allowing the boat to go head to wind. This is not the point. *Training to Win* is about winning races and every centimetre we can gain on a tack or gybe counts. It is just that the distance is greater / more noticeable with gybes.

The key to a good gybe is:

- Body movement
- Sheeting
- Steering

which are all done in sync. To improve this, you can stop doing one element (for example, put the sheet in the cleat!) to help you really focus on the other two.

Bum In The Boat

This is a very good exercise which can be done in surprisingly strong winds. It is class dependent, but the point is that the weight is not moved, so the sheeting and the steering need to be perfect. It is also a very good way to understand how to depower the boat because you cannot use your bodyweight to flatten the boat.

Ready to gybe when sailing with the bum in the boat

Difficulty	Exercise
Easy	Free sailing bum in the boat
Medium	Sail around a course bum in the boat
Hard	Racing bum in the boat

Race Strategy

Gybing is a vital part of race strategy. Long gone are the days where we just raced around triangles and the downwind leg was just how we got to the next upwind leg. It is now a good (perhaps the best) opportunity to gain places. Therefore, just like in the upwind leg, we need to gybe to get the gusts or the pressure as well as gybing on the shifts – here we want the headers, to take us as directly downwind as possible.

It is worth noting that there will be fewer shifts and gusts on the downwind leg than upwind because we are sailing away from them, rather than towards them. The pressure (a fixed area of stronger wind usually caused by a topographical feature) will remain in the same place.

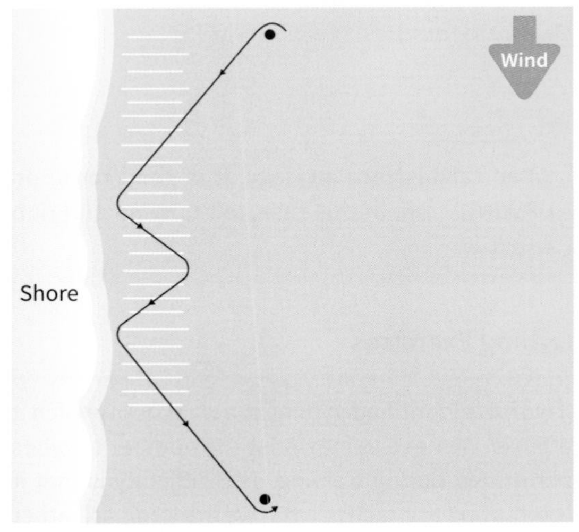

Gybe for the pressure because there is more wind by the shore when the shore is on the left in the Northern Hemisphere

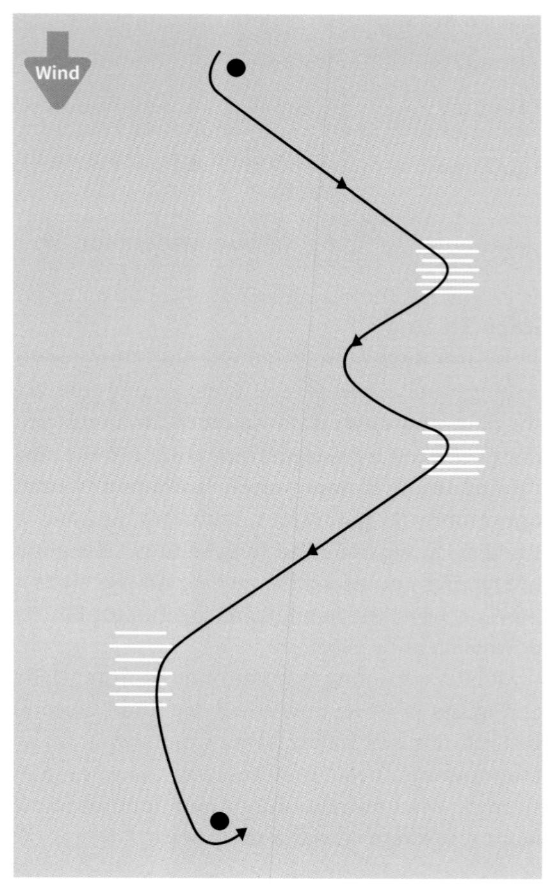

Gybe for the gusts

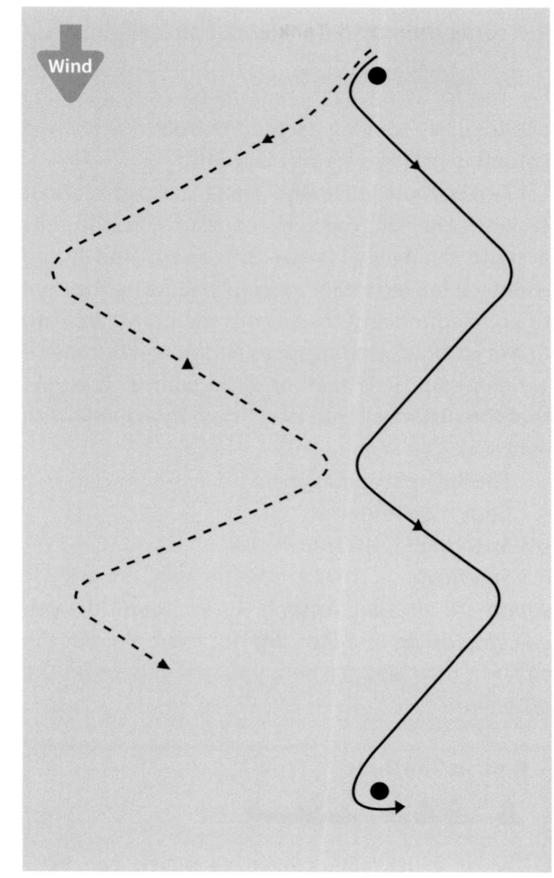

Gybe for the shifts and sail less distance

TOP TIP

When talking race strategy, it is good to be precise: 'There is more pressure on the left LOOKING UPWIND' – so, in this case, left upwind and right downwind would be good... everything else being equal.

Gybing Exercises

If we have identified gybing as a weakness (which it often is) we need to maximise the number of gybes performed during training. The difficulty is that it is tempting to practise what we are good at, rather than what we need to (because we are not so good at it). So, let's look at how we can add more gybes into our training sessions.

Three variations of the upwind exercises can work very well for sailing downwind and practising gybing.

In addition, when doing short races and someone is over the line, having to do one gybe upwind rather than going back through the line can be a suitable penalty for a premature start, because it is good to keep the racing as close as possible.

Gybing Upwind & Tacking Downwind

The first is that you change the upwind exercise so that you have to gybe rather than tack. Let me repeat that: when going upwind you have to gybe (no tacks allowed). You could also have it that you have to tack going downwind as well!

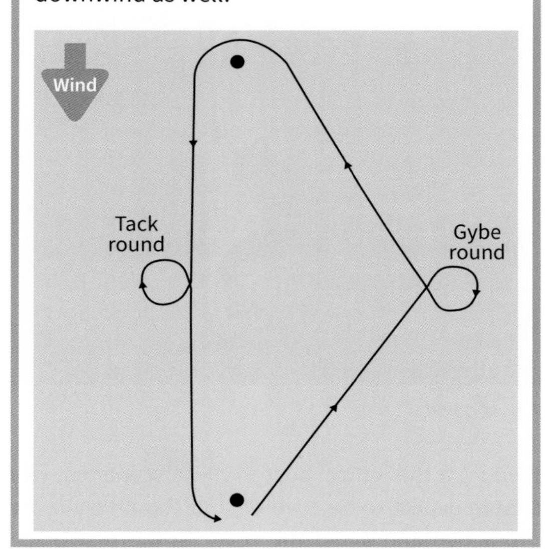

Triple Gybes & Triple Tacks

The other option is a triple gybe (when you want to gybe) and you could have to triple tack when going upwind.

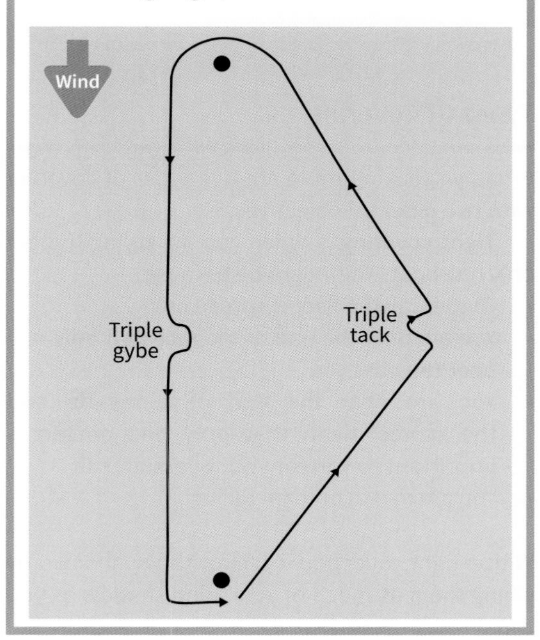

Different Tacks Downwind

In this exercise two boats start on opposite gybes downwind and gybe on the whistle. This is to see which, if any, gybe provides better VMG to the downwind mark and, particularly for single-handers, allow them to practise sailing on port gybe.

The feel of this is very different to racing when sailors usually get to choose when they will gybe, change angle etc. For example, sailors sailing with unstayed rigs may be very used to sailing downwind mainly on starboard tack because, from a rules point of view, you are safer. However, port tack may be faster because of the angle to waves or the ability to get to the wind you want etc. Sometimes it is hard to put a finger on the reason, but one tack is just faster!

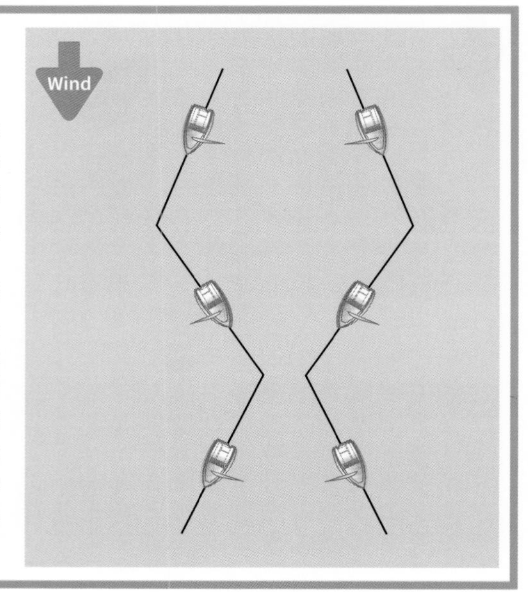

CHAPTER 5

Covering

Types Of Covering

Broadly speaking there are two types of covering with two different objectives.

Tight covering is when you are trying to beat only one boat. This might be because:

- Of the way the fleet is spread out
- You are near the end of the race and only one boat can pass you
- You are near the end of a regatta and the scores mean that only one person is important to you for your overall result
- You are match or team racing

A tight cover upwind

With a tight cover you will slow the rival down by giving them as much of your wind shadow as you can.

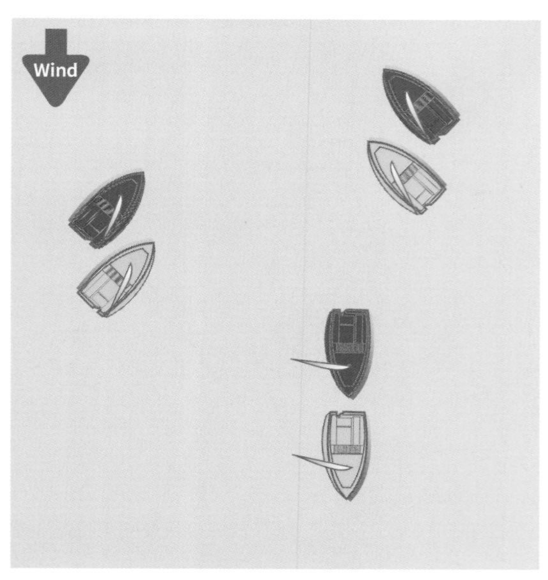

Tight cover (up and down wind)

If you are the 'other' boat in these scenarios, you should expect to be covered and should try to be pro-active and avoid the cover in the first place rather than trying to escape from it. It is easier to avoid the cover before it happens than to get out of it once it has been applied.

Loose covering is perhaps more common than close covering in fleet racing. In this case you are not giving them dirty air, but you are restricting their ability to make a gain on you.

It is about leverage. The greater the separation between you and the other boat, the greater the potential for gain or loss. So, for example, with a loose cover you go the same way as them up the beat, but do not take their wind otherwise they might tack, and you would separate.

The two types of cover are sometimes combined: you might choose to loose cover on one tack and tight cover on another to encourage them to sail on one side of you, for example in worse current, lighter winds or in more dirty air from other boats.

Loose cover

A loose cover upwind

A loose cover downwind

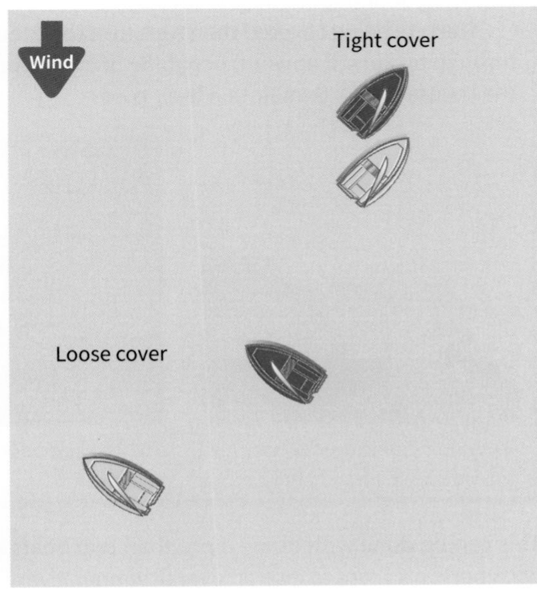

Tight and loose cover

Covering Exercises

Hopefully in regattas (because of your blistering speed!) you will rarely be covered and rarely need to cover, especially tight covering, but the infrequent occurrence means that it is even more important to practise this skill set so that you are ready for it when it happens.

These covering exercises work well with a boat-handling day, either doing normal racing first and then progressing to team / match racing, or the other way around (or a combination of the 2, as in the Match Race Within A Race).

Even more than when developing other skills, the exercises we need to do here are staged, or 'set up'. Where possible it works best with equal ability boats. In two-man boats you may consider swapping crews in order to really focus on each role (so a crew can crew for a variety of helms and a helm can helm for a variety of crews). The aim in most cases is for this to be a boat handling and tactics exercise rather than a boatspeed drag race to escape.

Attacker / Defender

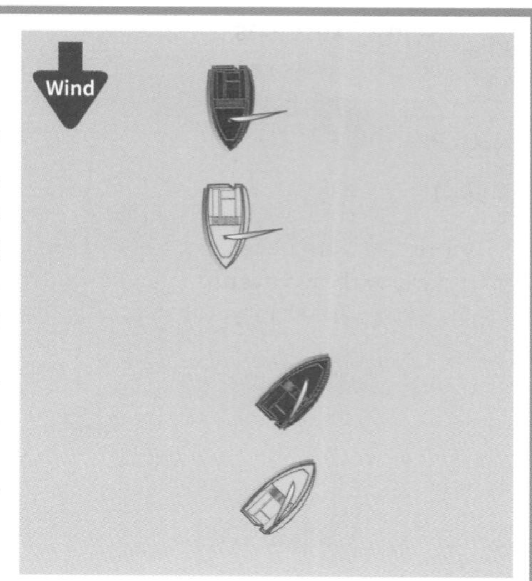

You can start this exercise from either a windward or leeward mark of the course. Before you get to the mark, start with Follow-My-Leader. The leader may take the other boat for a little bit of a dance: going fast, going slow, going fast again, trying to get a small advantage. This goes on until the mark is passed and then the covering begins.

If going upwind, the leader now applies a tight cover and the following boat is being covered; downwind the following boat applies a tight cover.

The one being covered then tries to escape the cover through tacking (if upwind) or gybing (if downwind) and the coverer seeks to maintain their cover.

Applying a tight cover upwind

The covered boat tries to break the cover

Applying a tight cover downwind

This can be done with many more than two boats and you can even make a little series of it, recording each person's score to give an overall winner. Every person has a go in each position and the lead person goes to the back. So, for example, the first order maybe 1,2,3,4,5,6 then the next race is 2,3,4,5,6,1 and the next 3,4,5,6,1,2 and so on.

Piggy-In-The-Middle

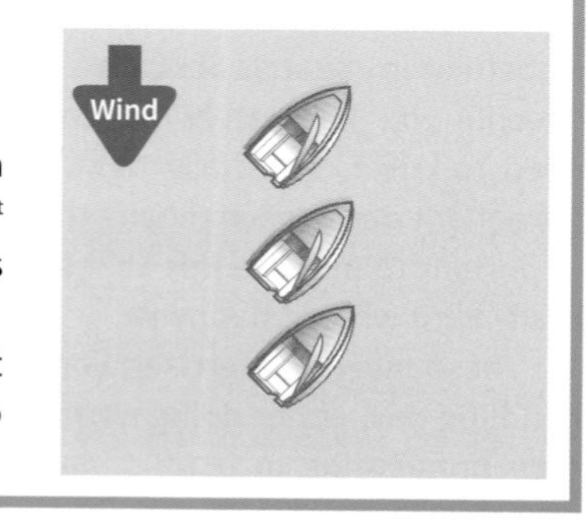

Piggy-In-The-Middle can be done on a small course or as a boatspeed exercise (with no turning marks involved). Here the 1st boat tries to push the 2nd boat to last place and allow the previous 3rd boat to get to 1st place at which point the exercise resets.

The 2nd boat's best defence is usually to try to hold the 3rd boat behind, although a big mistake by the 1st boat may allow them to overtake!

Match Racing Exercises

Match Race

A more complete covering exercise, particularly with two evenly matched boats, is to run a Match Race on a windward / leeward course.

At the 3-minute signal, one boat comes in on the starboard end of the line on starboard and the other comes in at the port end on port. The rules apply from this time. The one who gets the best of the start seeks to tight cover the other up the beat and then defend themselves from the cover downwind.

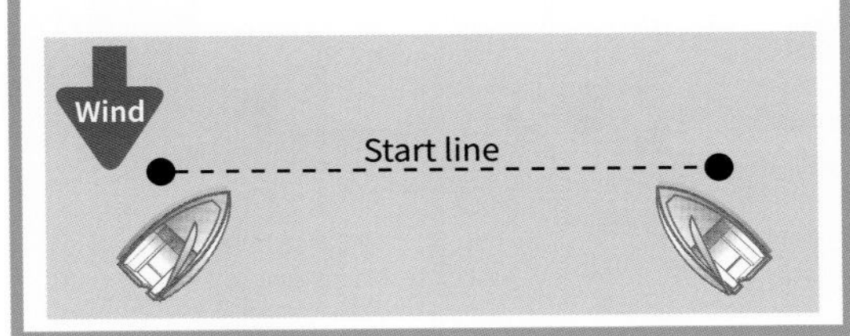

When the two boats start match racing can also be varied, just like in a real race where the boat-to-boat tactics change throughout the race. At the start, for example, everyone is close but towards the end maybe only 1 boat can pass. The objectives need to be clear: whether the aim is to slow the opposition down (tight cover) or simply to sail in a safe way to ensure that you stay ahead (loose cover).

Alternative times to start match racing are:

Match Race Within A Race

An alternative is, within a larger group, to identify two boats which will have a Match Race within the race that everyone else is participating in. These might be the more able, to allow them to get more out of the session, and may mean that they go slower and are therefore closer to the other boats.

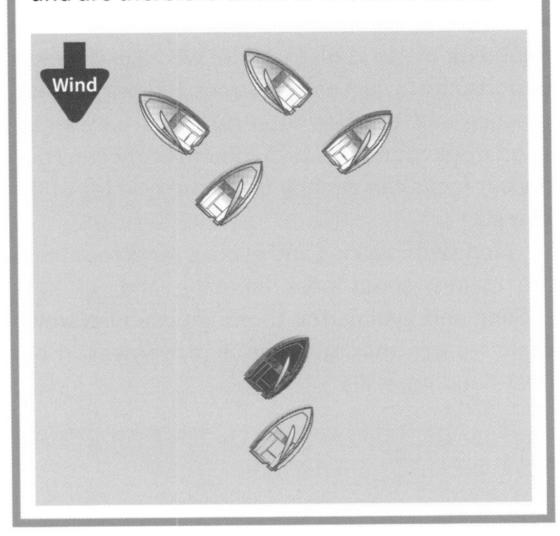

When they finish match racing can also be varied. As an alternative to just going to a conventional race finish, the race can keep going until someone is clear ahead. If they are clear ahead they can be challenged to do two 720s and still stay ahead. If they do, they carry on but with a tighter cover again. If they don't, the other boat now covers them.

Type of race	When start match racing
Full Match Race	From the 3-minute signal: port and starboard entry
Match Race from fleet race start	From the 3-minute signal
Normal start	Match Race starts after the start
Some point after start	Match Race starts at random point during the race (signalled by a whistle)
Final beat	Match Race starts on final beat

CHAPTER 6

Mark Rounding

The Importance Of Mark Rounding

Rounding marks is often where we have the most opportunity to gain or lose places. It takes practice, practice and practice to ensure that we can do good mark roundings with minimal concentration (so our focus can already be on the next leg of the course).

Along with tacking and gybing, mark roundings are mainly about boat handling and, as with tacking and gybing, the thorough use of planned exercises can maximise the improvement in our boat-handling skills.

The windward mark can get very crowded

However, mark roundings are about more than just boat handling: there are also:

- Tactical considerations: how to use the rounding to improve your position compared to the opposition
- Strategic considerations: situations can change very quickly, and we need to plan ahead
- Rules considerations: mark roundings are also the place where we often see the greatest number of protests

As can the leeward mark

But it is boat handling that is critical – there is no point in knowing the rules if you can't handle your boat to abide by them!

Marks can be rounded in two ways:

- Heading up into the wind (for example, run to reach, reach to beat)
- Bearing away from the wind (for example, beat to reach, beat to run, reach to run)

All of these will occur on a typical course, usually in a set direction, but it is also important, if we are to be a complete athlete, to practise manoeuvres that we may not do that often. For example, we should practise starboard windward mark roundings, bearing away on port tack, hoisting on port tack, etc. We develop stronger muscle memory by practising both ways and the increased use of gates instead of single turning marks in races means that there is now often a choice of rounding.

Alternate Mark Roundings

Set up a windward / leeward course (without a gate, to force specific mark roundings) and alternate the way the turning marks are rounded each lap.

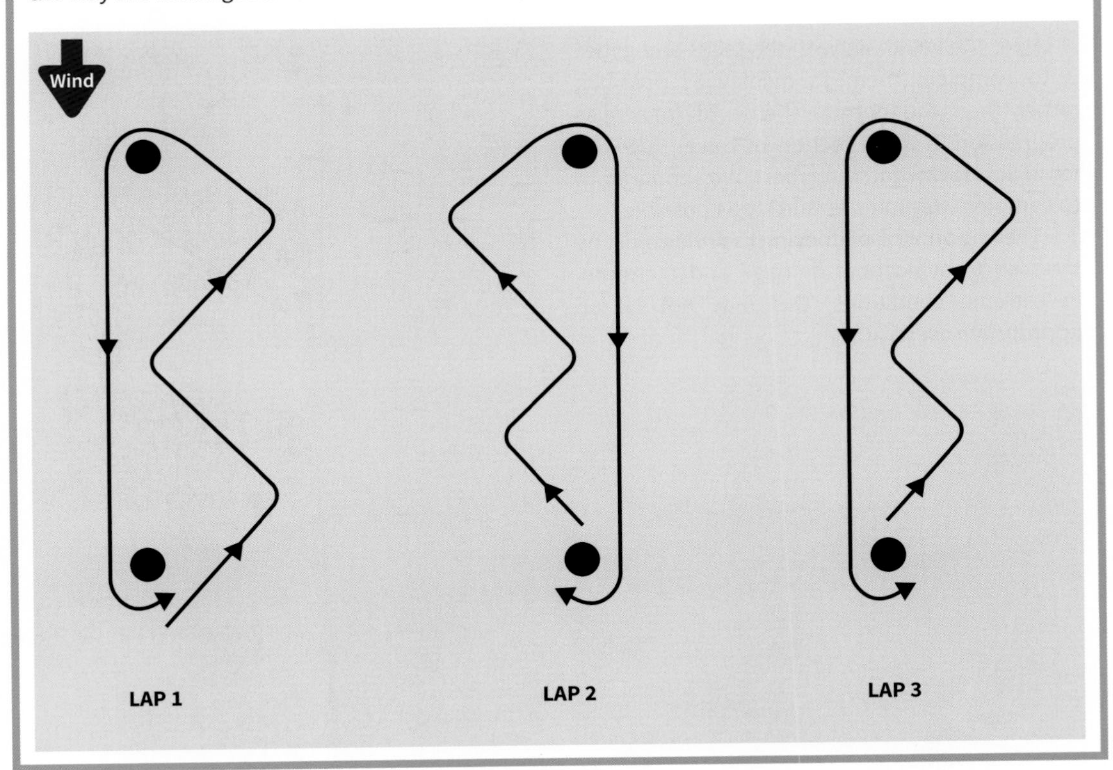

Still within the idea of practising things we don't do very often, there are some things that we don't generally do in a race:

- We rarely tack off immediately at the leeward mark / gate as this means we sail through the fleet sailing downwind.
- Likewise, at a windward mark we will rarely gybe as this may mean we sail back through the upwind boats.
- In single-handed boats, like the Laser, people rarely go downwind on port because starboard seems 'safer' rules wise.

However sometimes these will be the best option due to the angle of the wave / breeze / current, but if you never practise them they can seem unfamiliar and therefore slower, so we do need to practise them so that we can do them (when required) in racing.

So, to make the rounding more difficult, gybe just before the leeward mark and tack just before the windward mark and leave adjustment of sail controls until the last possible minute. You can also gybe and tack immediately after the mark, which puts additional pressure on.

Gut Buster

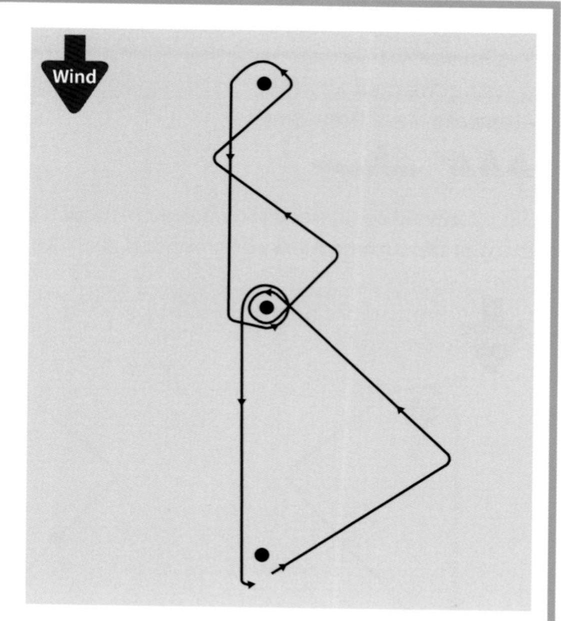

I have to say this is one of my favourite exercises. You set a windward / leeward course with a buoy in the middle which has to be rounded: both upwind and downwind. When rounding you also have to raise and drop the spinnaker, if you have one.

Here the key thing with the tacks and gybes is to complete them as quickly as possible, rather than the normal theme of 'maximise progression in the direction of travel' (upwind for tacks, downwind for gybes). We simply want to complete the spins as quickly as possible.

The importance of obeying the rules must be stressed to avoid boat damage and therefore, in extreme conditions, this may not be an appropriate exercise.

In the Gut Buster you round a mark in the middle of the beat

A variation of this is to blow a whistle for the boats to complete a 720° turn but, in my experience, this is never as focused an exercise as the Gut Buster.

However, we can still use the 720 if someone gets too far ahead of the group, in a race, to bring them back together and keep the racing close.

Progression

Increasing the difficulty is very important when it comes to boat-handling training: the more difficult the exercise, the easier it will make winning on the race course. You must always push your comfort levels; confidence as well as competence is very important. For example, if you train in 30 knots, suddenly racing in 25 knots seems much easier.

So, with the alternate mark roundings, we can look at altering the rounding every lap (after the first). Here are 3 examples:

1. Different Rounding Windward & Leeward:

	Windward mark rounding	Leeward mark rounding
Lap 1	Port	Port
Lap 2	Starboard	Port
Lap 3	Port	Starboard
Repeat even laps	Starboard	Port
Repeat odd laps	Port	Starboard

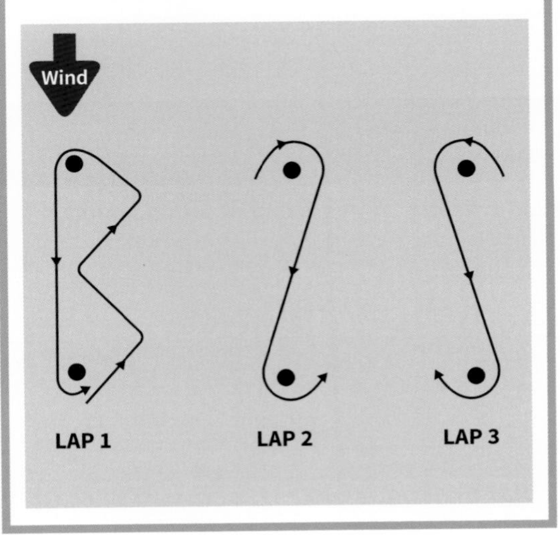

2. Same Windward (can be done either port or starboard, this time shown as port) **But Leeward Mark Changes:**

	Windward mark rounding	Leeward mark rounding
Lap 1	Port	Port
Lap 2	Port	Starboard
Lap 3	Port	Port
Repeat even laps	Port	Starboard
Repeat odd laps	Port	Port

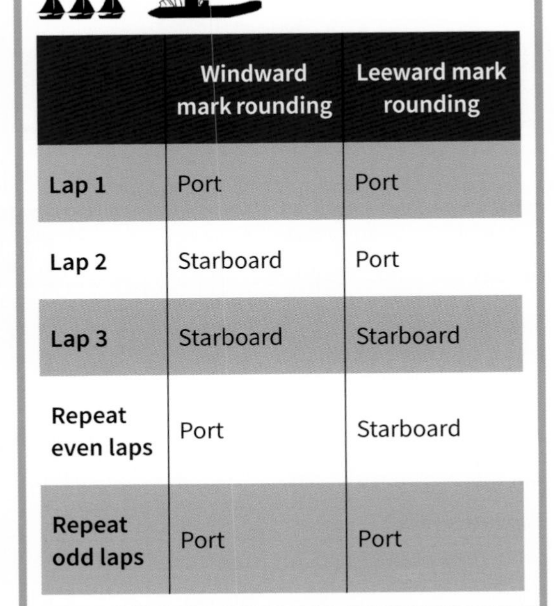

3. Or the more complex, Change One Mark At A Time:

	Windward mark rounding	Leeward mark rounding
Lap 1	Port	Port
Lap 2	Starboard	Port
Lap 3	Starboard	Starboard
Repeat even laps	Port	Starboard
Repeat odd laps	Port	Port

One of the key things with short course racing in training is 'add-ons' like this. They make the exercise harder, meaning that you push yourself harder and the potential benefit is greater. However, you want to avoid training where you set yourself up to fail, either due to training when too fatigued or when an exercise is too difficult (maybe 35+ knots or whatever the same limit for your class is).

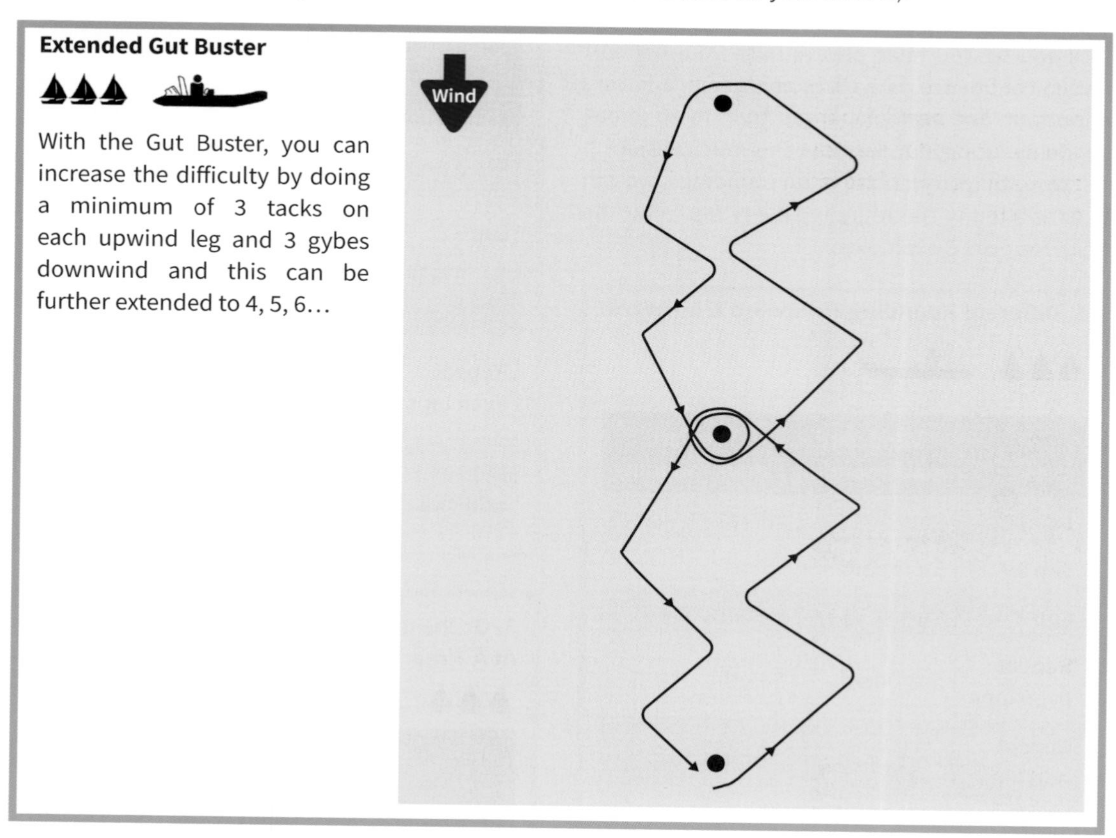

Extended Gut Buster

With the Gut Buster, you can increase the difficulty by doing a minimum of 3 tacks on each upwind leg and 3 gybes downwind and this can be further extended to 4, 5, 6…

Increasing the difficulty of the Gut Buster:

	More difficult	Less difficult
Gut Buster	More rounds around middle buoy	Less rounds around middle buoy
Windward leg	Shorter	Longer
Tacks	More	Less
Downwind leg	Shorter	Longer
Gybes	More	Less

Tight Circles

Gut Busters and 720s are a great warm-up but a very simple and good exercise you can do on your own is simply tight circles. You need to push yourself to do the tightest possible circle you can for the available wind strength and bearing in the mind how much alteration you are doing (for example is the centreboard staying down and you just do the mainsheet or are you aiming to trim the boat perfectly).

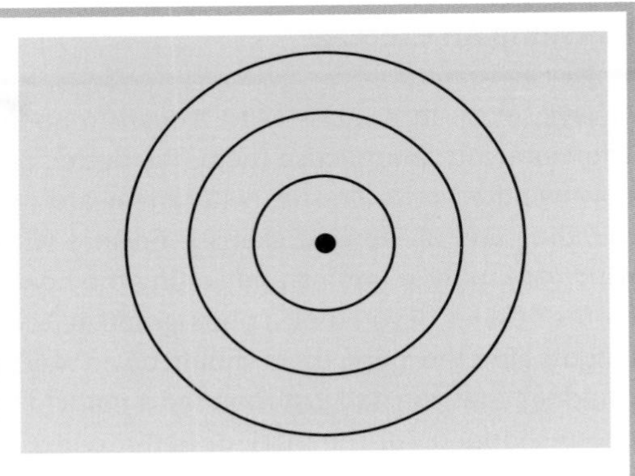

Try to do as tight a circle as you can

	Circle	Action	Aim
1	Super tight	Just mainsheet and body movement	Closest possible circle
2	Tight	Sail controls on / off	Practice for adjusting sail controls and simulated mark rounding
3	Tight as you can!!!	All equipment in normal position, including spinnaker hoists and drops	In a photo it would look like normal racing trim: the ultimate boat-handling exercise

Finishing An Exercise

Always finish an exercise with a mark rounding. The more you can practise them, the better. So, a downwind exercise finishes with a leeward mark rounding and an upwind exercise finishes with a windward mark rounding and setting the boat up for the next leg. If you took a photograph at 3 boat-lengths after the mark, there should be no way you could tell that you had just rounded a mark (if you photo-shopped out the mark or had it out of the picture).

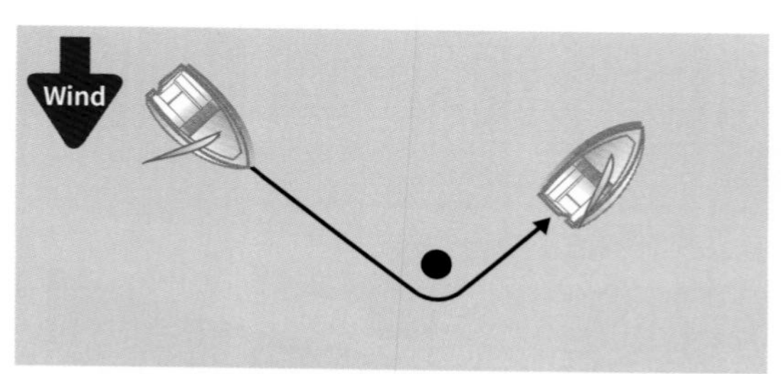

Leeward finish: Do the rounding and sail a few boat lengths before stopping

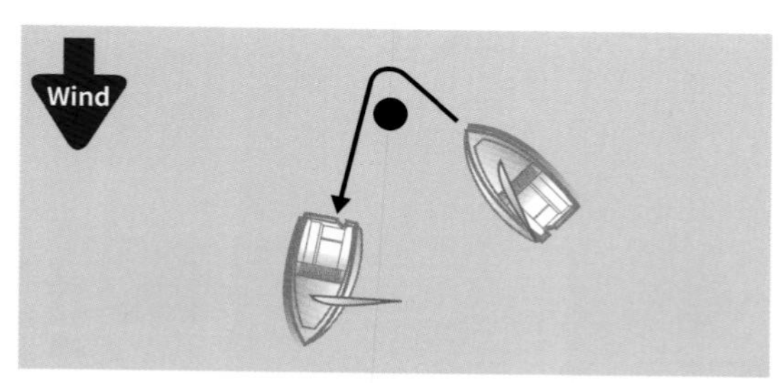

Windward finish: Do the rounding and set the sails for the next leg before stopping

In the absence of a mark at the end of an exercise, still go through the process of adjusting sail controls, doing a good head up or bear away and sail the next leg at full speed (to check correct adjustments have been made) for at least a couple of boat lengths.

Then you must rest because you cannot go full-on in a race and then do a poor mark rounding, so you need to get in the habit of giving yourself just enough time.

To push further, either when finishing or during a short course race, practise the immediate boat handling manoeuvres (tack at leeward mark or gybe at windward mark). You may need to do this in a race to escape cover or simply to get to the favoured side of the course.

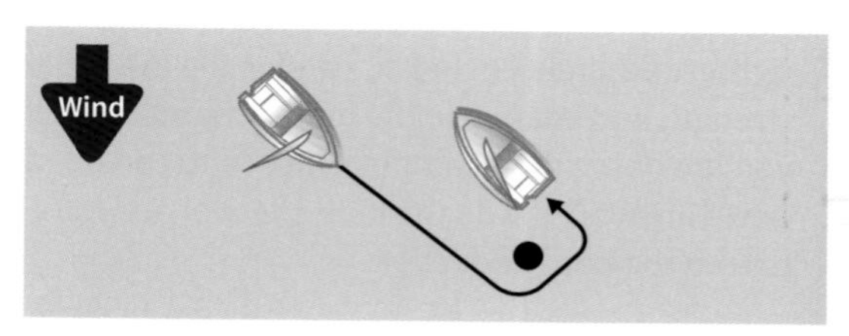

Leeward finish: Do the rounding and then tack immediately

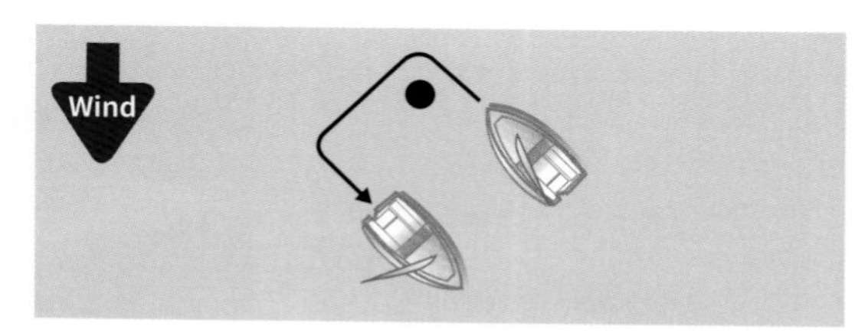

Windward finish: Do the rounding and then gybe immediately

When finishing with a downwind gate, boats should immediately tack and cross to see who really picked the favoured gate mark to round (the one who crosses ahead). Try to do any analysis soon after the exercise is complete, so learning can be processed as soon as possible.

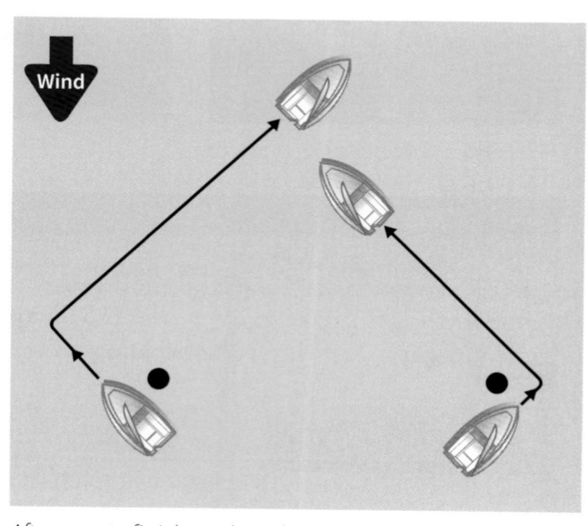

After a gate finish: tack and cross

CHAPTER 7
Upwind

Key Elements Upwind

In many classes (but certainly not all), the upwind may be the most physically demanding, and gaining specific fitness in this area is key. The fitter you are the harder you can work and the easier it is to concentrate on the racing, so we have some sessions which are specifically designed to improve fitness. That means a volume of continuous training where rest is minimised, and the session is not broken down into up and downwind. (When racing you do get rest between races, but if you train hard, with minimal rest, it will make the racing easier.)

First things first! The order that you do your training in is very important. For example, if you have a very hard sailing session to do (strong winds or you know it will be a long session) you need to do this first, while you are fully focused, and other sessions like a light aerobic or core session can be done later. We need to make sure that we are learning good habits and always sailing in good form. This is not only fast, it also protects the body from injury which could occur with training when overtired.

Sailing upwind is physically demanding and needs fitness

After a hard upwind session, recovery is especially vital – see chapter 10 on Fitness.

Another key area upwind (which fitness obviously contributes to), particularly in dinghies, is keeping the boat flat. This is best achieved through a combination of 3 things:

- Hiking / trapezing
- Sheeting
- Steering

If you leave out one of these elements, then you have to be far more precise with the remaining two. For example, if you are hiking / trapezing 'flat out' with the sails 'fully in' you need very good steering.

Upwind Exercises

When practising upwind work, it is very important that the windward mark, whether this is a buoy or a coach boat, is anchored so the sailors can also learn to judge laylines. If you do lots of practice with drifting buoys or RIBs as marks you may find that, when actually racing, the sailors will tend to tack under the laylines as they are used to the buoy / RIB travelling downwind (when they are not fixed).

Stepping Stone Upwind

Sail to the windward mark, and round correctly, sail downwind for 2 boat lengths with sail controls etc. fully adjusted for the downwind and then stop. Then use a Rabbit Start to start again upwind to a new windward mark which you round, sail downwind for 2 boat lengths and then stop. And then repeat with another Rabbit Start and upwind leg to a new windward mark, and so on.

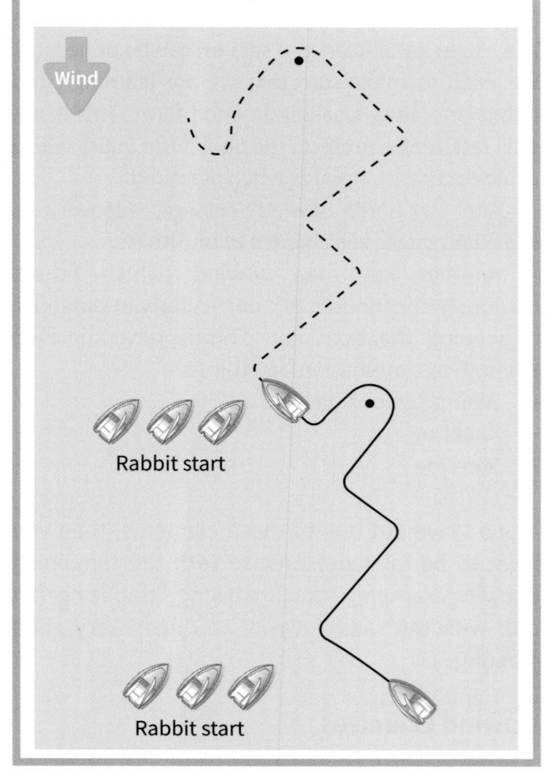

Keelboat-Style Steering

Going fast in any boat is about steering the optimum angle to the next mark and so this is a good exercise to focus on steering, separate from the other elements of hiking / trapezing and trimming we discussed earlier. It is all too easy to steer too much or just use all your bodyweight to 'bully' the boat around the course, especially if you are young and fit. So, in this exercise, you sit 'keelboat-style': sitting on the side deck but in reverse, with your legs pointing out (be careful not to drag your feet in the water as it will slow you down). This means that your body weight is fixed and it may even be hard to sheet. This makes good steering suddenly the main focus of your attention.

Sailing keelboat-style

This exercise could also be used as a way of progressing to the intended race area rather than towing, or an extended warm-up for getting to a race area, or a way of taking people back to shore and keeping them focused.

Depending upon the venue, it may be extremely important to train on the precise race area to experience the same currents, waves, wind, etc.

This exercise can be easy or difficult:

Easy	Free sailing keelboat style
Medium	Sail around a course keelboat style
Hard	Racing keelboat style

Standing Up Racing

To sail fast, boat balance is key, and you can steer the boat through your feet by weighting them or by using the toestrap (either pulling on the front or back foot). When standing you can see precisely the best positioning of weight for optimum speed and boat handling, and it also encourages smooth sheeting and steering (especially in 2-man boats where you have to work together). Jerky steering or sheeting may cause someone to fall over! The more you are standing straight, with feet close together (rather than crouching down with your feet well apart) the harder, and therefore better, this exercise is.

Standing racing

Another exercise for upwind speed is the Lane Hold, described on p26.

Getting Your Head Out Of The Boat

While we can (and should) work on our boatspeed, sailboat racing is not simply a drag race where whoever is fastest wins the race. Sailing is more like orienteering. You run as fast as you can, whilst looking at a map to choose the best route. You need to be going fast AND in the correct direction.

When training upwind we also need to keep heads out of the boat. I have often seen the fastest boat in a straight line in a training session struggle in racing because the focus is too internal.

Offset Marks / Finish

Having offset marks or even an offset windward finish (all ready to start another exercise) can help with this, or you could move the position of marks during the exercise.

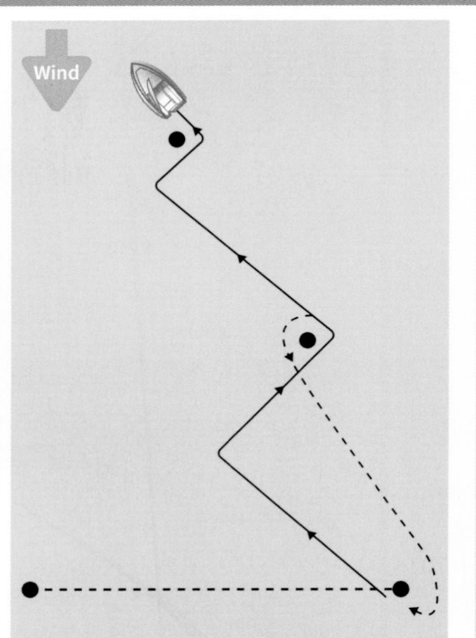

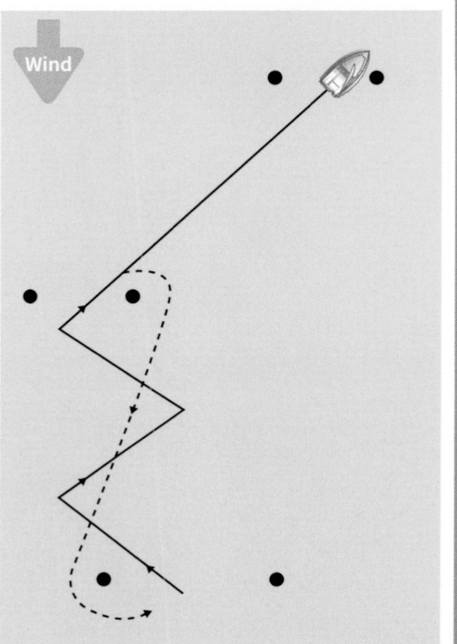

Delayed Mark Setting

Alternatively, the marks / finish line could be dropped only after the start to make the sailors really look. In a race they need to be able to assess which end of a line is better due to distance sailed and any line bias, while keeping good boatspeed and minimising the number of tacks.

Another way to get sailors to examine the course area constantly is to have the RIB acting as a windward mark, but continually moving until finally anchoring (and blowing a whistle or raising a hand to make it clear that it is now in a fixed position). This requires thinking ahead and good communication between the crew(s) and helm.

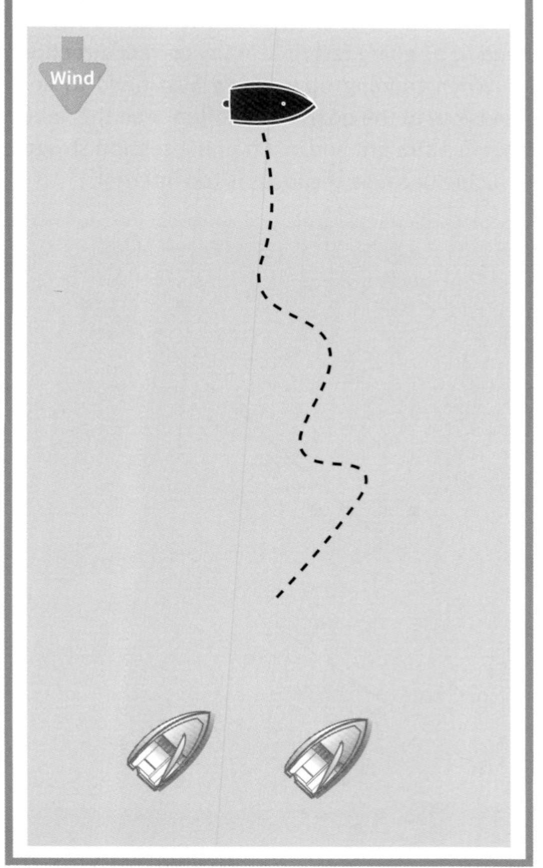

TOP TIP

In a regatta a good way to test the course is to split tacks with someone who is a very similar speed to you. For example, if you have time and it is approximately a 16-minute beat you can do a Rabbit Start on port / starboard and then sail for 4 minutes and tack, then 8 minutes and tack, then 4 minutes and tack and see who is gaining at which cross point and then have a conversation as to why. (If you have less time or a smaller course you could of course do 2-minute splits for example.)

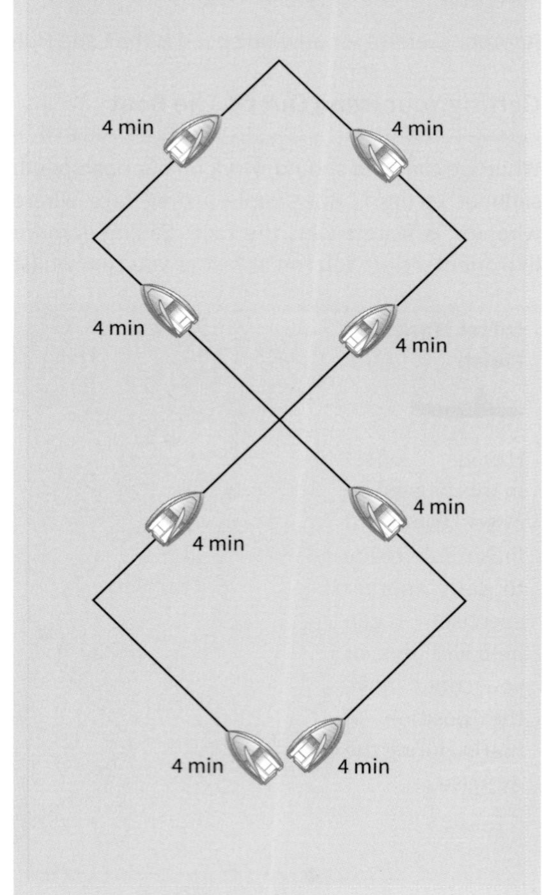

Split tacks course testing

CHAPTER 8
Reaching

Reaching needs focus, as we need to be very clear where we are trying to get to. That is not just going for maximum speed but maximum velocity made good (VMG) to the next mark. It is very tempting to go for maximum speed, but this may mean that we end up sailing at a slower speed near the end of the leg. As always, considering the big picture and any tidal / pressure difference is key. After all it is lots of fun to go reaching around at top speed (as a lot of leisure windsurfers do) but the purpose of this book is to make you better racers.

When reaching, at every point, you need to think about what you are trying to do:

- Get high
- Get low
- Get on the plane
- Get on a wave

Which of these you are trying to do at any point in time is often related to the VMG. For example:

- If you are going as low as possible while still surfing, then you are maximising your gain (as you will be faster when you head up)
- If you get the boat going at maximum planing speed, then bear away as much as you can. While maintaining speed you are therefore maximising your gain (by going down in gusts and up in lulls)
- Assuming medium wind, take as much power as you can, and only lose power when it is causing you drag (light winds) or you are over-powered (stronger winds). Generally, the harder you work the faster you go!

You can monitor this progress by recording your speed and track using GPS. (You can also monitor your physical work rate with a heart rate monitor.)

Reaching covers a huge range of angles to the wind. The closer the reach is to a beat the more the sailing style and aims resemble those of a beat, and similarly for broad reaching and the run. When close to the wind, in some cases, it may be faster to carry on almost beating in order to get a better reaching angle (or dropping the spinnaker early for the same reason).

Basic Reaching Exercises

We want to make the most of every minute of training; just think how close the finishes of some races are or Championships are on points – maybe everything coming down to who beat whom in the final race. The key idea is that from the moment we hit the water we want to be working hard and efficiently; and no one has to wait for anyone else before their training can commence.

Follow-My-Leader (see p17) is a great exercise to keep the group together with the boats who launch later having to reach as soon as possible to join the back of the group.

Moving Reaching Mark

Another way to bring everyone together and keep the reaching very tight is to frequently change the position of the mark. At one point you may be too high or too low of the mark and suddenly that changes, or perhaps you were the inside boat and the RIB moves and now you are the outside boat. Learning to 'keep your head out of the boat' is key.

Catch The Coach Boat

A simpler variation on this is for the coach boat to set off 'on a reach' and then go higher or lower and the sailors following have to follow the coach boat. The coach boat can then stop and be used as a rounding mark to give practice on lots of different legs.

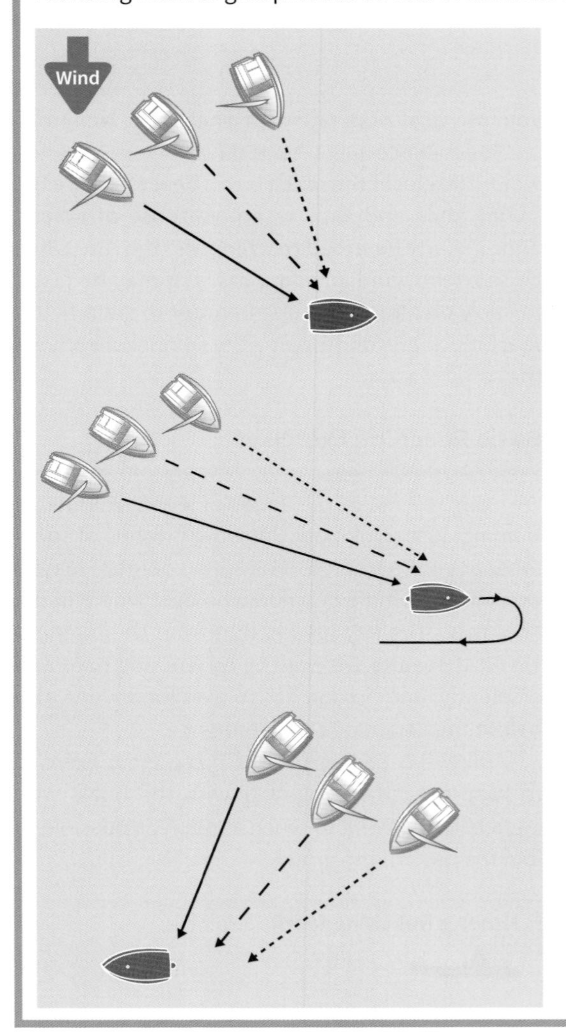

Catch the coach boat

The coach boat can also act as a turning mark

There are many variations that can be built into these exercises. For example, a slalom type course, where the marks are constantly moved between laps, not only gets the focus on velocity made good (VMG) but encourages head-out-of-the-boat sailing too.

Advanced Exercises

As mentioned before, it is often said that when you lose one of your senses (e.g. sight) then your other senses (e.g. hearing) are heightened. This is certainly true in sailing and so these exercises are about removing one sense so that the other senses are heightened.

These exercises have been placed in the reaching chapter because reaching is very much about feel. However, as a progression, they can be done both up and downwind and may even be included in a race. Generally speaking, the level of difficulty is something like this:

Difficulty level* (out of 10)	Task
2	Reaching
5	Beating
7	Running
8	Full race course (Beating, Reaching and Running)

* This will also be affected by wind speed, wave size and length of leg.

When moving to the full race course it can be done on a triangle / sausage or trapezoid course.

No Hearing

You may be surprised but it is not only through sight that we assess the wind and waves for steering, sheeting and body movement. We also listen to the hull noise (slamming and banging or smooth as silk). This is a good one to try along with Blind-Folded Sailing as, when blindfolded, you will have been more aware of your hearing. A good set of noise-cancelling head phones will do the trick.

Racing without being able to hear

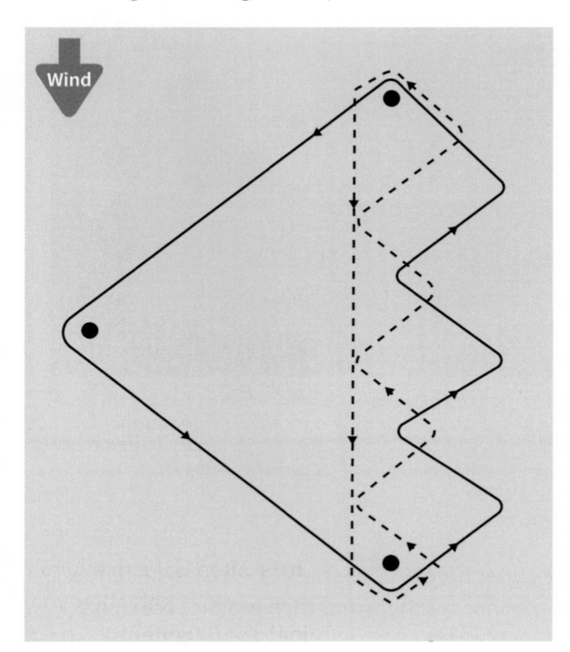

Triangle / sausage course

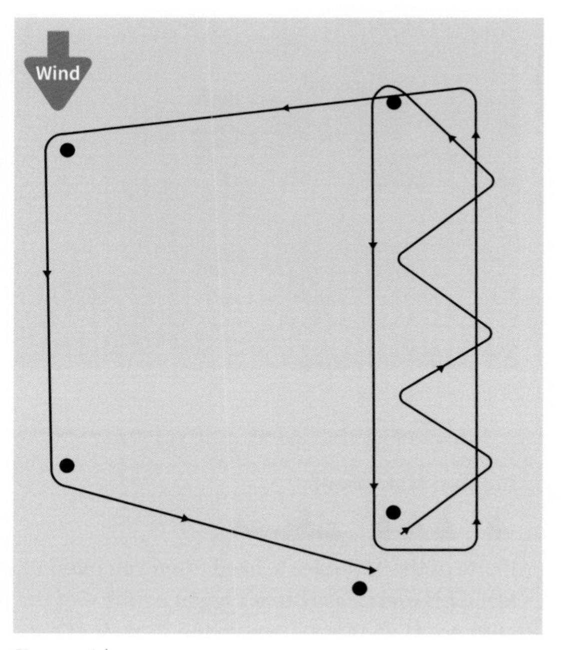

Trapezoid course

Blind-Folded Sailing

Nothing can help you focus on the course made good as having to do it without looking. This is one of the more difficult exercises, so starting with just reaching is a good idea before progressing onto beating and running, and finally, with active support from a coach boat (telling you when to tack and gybe) you can even race.

The entry level for this exercise is just looking behind you and thinking about balance. You can then build up to the time you close your eyes. The tendency is often to load up the rig (for example sail heeled upwind or hard by the lee downwind in a single-hander) but this is not the fast way.

Initially it should start as an individual exercise but there is no reason why you cannot do speed work, or even boat handling exercises (like Tacking On The Whistle).

Sailing when looking astern

Sailing blind-folded

Cleated Mainsheet

If one of the variables is fixed, then you need to work super hard on the others. Precision becomes key. This exercise is done 1 leg at a time. Set the mainsail for reaching and then practise reaching with no adjustment, then do the same for beating, then running.

Boat Balance

There are two options here:

- Standing Up helps with balance and agility
- Bum In The Boat is all about power control because you cannot move to balance the boat

Again, start with reaching before progressing to other points of sailing.

Racing when standing

Racing with bum in the boat

These exercises are very different because one (Standing Up Racing) is about managing boat balance precisely with the body, whereas the other (Bum In The Boat) is about the body having no contribution to boat balance. So they are not alternatives, but practising different things.

They work with the dead downwind sailing because the pressure of the wind is directly behind, so there is no issue with the boat being over or under powered.

In contrast to the No Hearing exercise you can have direct communication with the coach – not allowed in racing, but very good in training. The sailor has a waterproof microphone and headset and can continually talk to the coach, just like a Formula 1 driver can talk to his team.

If you do the Blind-folded Sailing exercise, make sure the coach videos it because the sailors are always very interested to see what really happened.

Controlled Tiller

These exercises remove the tiller from your control – again forcing you to concentrate more on the other things that you can control. For reaching there are several variations of this:

1. Rudder up completely
2. Tiller not held but able to move freely
3. Tiller restrained, so that it can move only a limited amount (remember huge tiller movements can act like a brake)
4. Tiller tied (so not able to move)

Racing with no rudder

Racing with the tiller tied

CHAPTER 9

Downwind

Many of the most important races are now decided on a windward / leeward course and even on a trapezoid course most of the place changes are likely to occur on the upwind and downwind legs. Also, with many races now finishing near the leeward mark, the importance of downwind speed has increased dramatically in many classes of boat, as has the sailors' fitness to really work the boat downwind.

We can gradually increase the distance sailed downwind as sailors' focus and fitness allows the exercise to become more demanding. We can even do long purely downwind sessions by towing upwind and then just sailing downwind (or, depending upon the wind direction, sailing downwind and then towing back). (See p18 for more details on towing.)

Please note: diagrams are single-sailed for clarity. Many boats will be using more than 1 sail downwind and careful trimming of all three sails will contribute to achieving maximum boatspeed.

Basic Downwind Exercises

If the training area (or home) is not directly downwind you can also break the exercise down by doing dead downwind, small reach, dead downwind etc. Try to practise dead downwind and the common reaching angles sailed by your class.

It is important to have a mark to go to, to provide race-like focus and be a true test of who has the best VMG. For example, it may be easier to surf the waves in one direction while you will need to work very hard to surf in the other. This will only become obvious when you go to a mark because the sailors who can best surf the waves in the

Stepping Stone Downwind

Just like the upwind progression we can use repeat marks downwind to either begin or end a session. We need to try to make the course as true downwind as possible allowing for changes in wind direction and the effect of the current. Please note this is often different from the straight down wave direction!

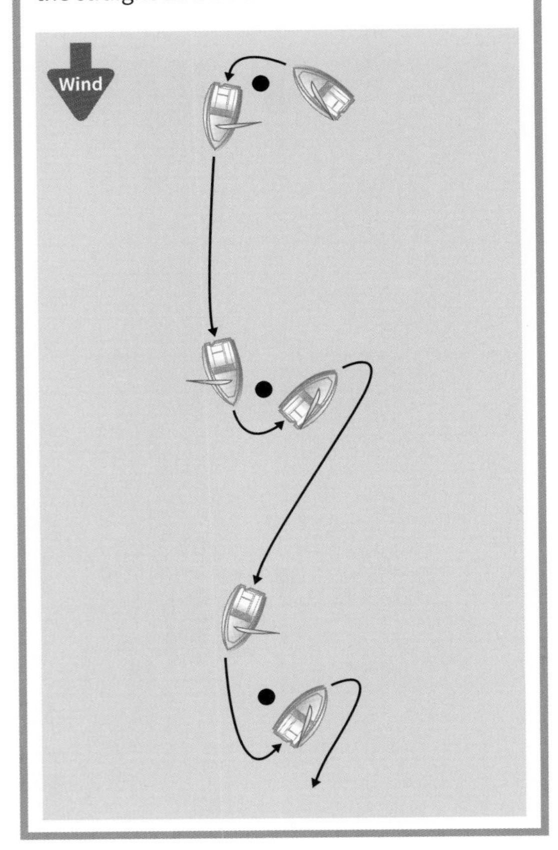

difficult direction are likely to be first to the mark.

Each mark must be rounded correctly with the sail controls adjusted and the boat fully set up for the upwind leg before stopping. A good leeward mark rounding is a vital race skill and should be practised at every opportunity.

Gradually Increasing Leg Length

One way of gradually lengthening the course would be to anchor the windward mark and allow the leeward mark to drift gradually downwind. (If there was strong current going upwind then you would do the opposite: anchor the leeward mark and allow the windward mark to be carried by the current upwind.) For obvious reasons this does not work well if the current is 'side on'.

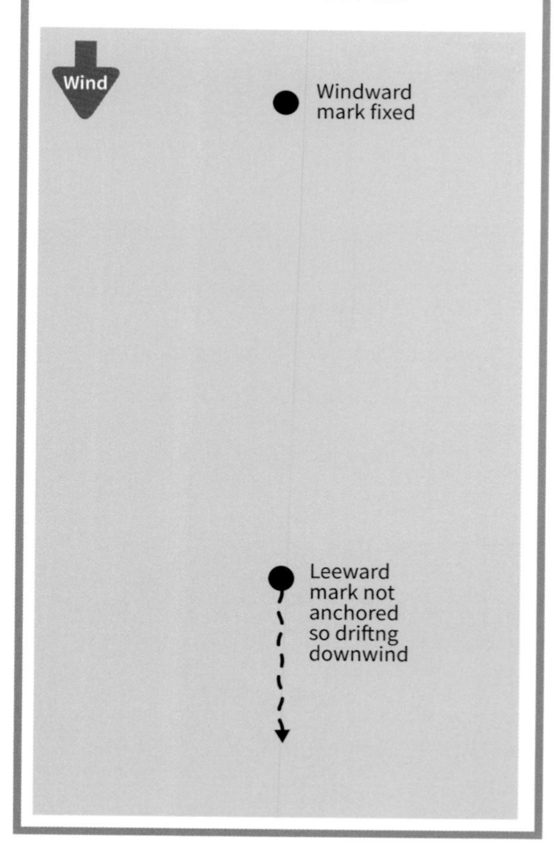

Feel

Downwind sailing is very much about feel. You shouldn't be forcing the boat to do things with the rudder; rather you should be making the boat want to do what you want it to do with the boat balance and sheeting (although these actions may be very physical). So, you are the drill instructor making the boat do what you want, but the way you deliver the message needs to be done in a way which will not create resistance. After all, if you pull hard on the rudder, it can act as a brake.

The reason feel is so important is that you are always trying to push yourself.

Upwind you need to be working your maximum to flatten the boat and steer around the waves. The boat needs to have some bite and, if you didn't work full out, it would want to head up. The only slight rest is in the flat spots (no waves) or lulls (if already fully powered up and footing).

Downwind must seem the same: the boat is always trying to surge downwind, and is probably quite unstable. The rig should be set up making it easy to steer (both head up and bear away). If you end up fighting the boat, it is rarely fast. And, therefore, training exercises must reflect this.

The key points are:

- Think ahead (don't just look at the wave ahead, look 3 waves ahead and plan your route)
- Communicate (everyone must know the plan)
- Begin with the desired end result in mind (because otherwise it is very easy to end up too far left or right on the course, in the dirty area of the chasing pack, gybing too late etc.)

Rudderless Sailing / Controlled Tiller

One of the best exercises for this is rudderless sailing in 2-man boats or tied tiller in most single-handers. If one or more boats are very good at this, you can even get them to do a 360 or even 720 in the race to slow them down and keep everyone together... normal racing rules apply. It should be possible to put the rudder back down or untie the tiller super quick just in case.

Running with no rudder

- The easy version of this is simply to start sailing downwind and when everything is balanced. Tie the tiller or raise the rudder.
- The next progression is to sail around a course, perhaps 'triangle / sausage' so you practise beating, reaching and running.
- The hardest version is to do a proper race, especially on a short course in strong winds!

Racing with the rudder tied

Boat Balance

Standing Up Racing

One of the best ways of improving your boatspeed is to work on your boat balance and one of the best ways to achieve this is to practise standing. Here a sudden drop of the sheet or jerky steering may make you fall over. You learn to be smooth and controlled and to think ahead. It is also good for understanding weight positioning for speed, as you can be precise with your feet, standing in exactly the best place to maximise speed.

Let it be clear, this is a standing exercise, not standing on one leg, not crouching down. You should be standing straight and tall at all times: like a soldier on duty. The only time you are allowed to duck is when the boom passes over (in a tack or gybe). The rest of the time you are standing correctly… so, if I took a photo and 'photo-shopped' you from standing in the boat to standing somewhere else, nothing would look unusual apart from the fact you were wearing sailing clothes in the middle of the High Street!

Running while standing

The progression for this exercise is:

Easy	Free sailing standing
Medium	Sail around a course standing
Hard	Racing standing

TOP TIP

Lightweight footwear is a must, so you can feel the boat through the soles of your shoes, or the toestrap. The more 'locked in' to the boat you are the better, as any movements you make will be better translated to the boat. You may even want shoes which feel slightly too tight on land, so they are perfect on the water (when wet and hiking, the action tends to pull the boot off your feet). Sailing shoes are also 'dead weight' because they are always inside the boat, so you should be very keen to keep this to a minimum.

Lightweight and supportive footwear is essential

Other Downwind Exercises

Downwind Starts

In all the exercises we are trying to make them as race-like as possible, so by starting the boats close together we achieve this feel. It is much harder to sail fast when surrounded by a group of boats than on your own. When racing, we will spend a lot of time surrounded by other boats. It is our ability to finish at the front of the pack, or pull through the fleet, which is most likely to determine our regatta finishing position, not how much we can win a race by when we get away. So, it is best to practise surrounded by other boats. Of course, normal racing rules apply for all these races.

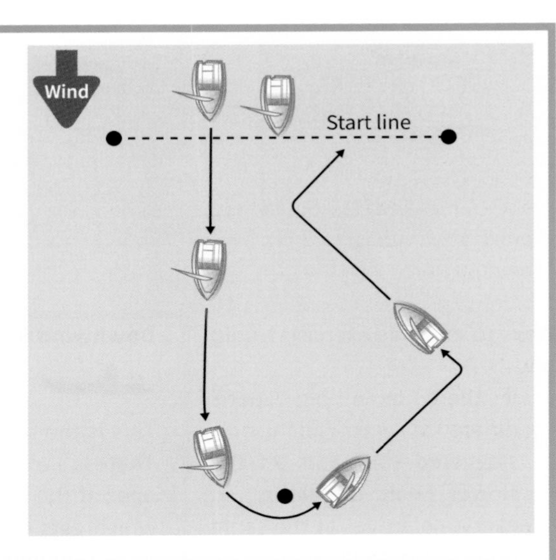

Downwind start

This will involve everyone sailing on a run and working on their boatspeed. You could start this with the downwind start (as described above). Alternatively, you could start without a start line, with everyone lined up on a reach. The simplest way would be for everyone to bear away on a whistle but simplest is not always best. We want to make the most of every minute of every training session so, if we can combine two skill sets in one exercise, then why not? So, line up on a reach and then, on the whistle, tack before going downwind. This head up, tack and bear away is great boat handling practice as it is much more difficult than just bearing away, especially in strong winds.

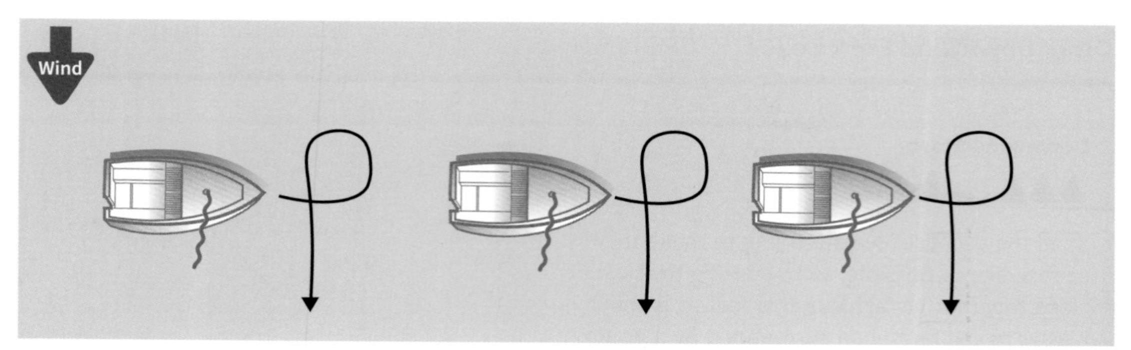

Alternative start

Ways to end this exercise would be:

- If there is a big speed difference you can use a staggered start and set the slower boats off earlier, so everyone arrives at the same time
- Finish the exercise with three gybes
- You can do a Downwind Riverboat where sailors have to stay inside a downwind triangle

TOP TIP

To end the exercises: always round a leeward mark (doing a good spinnaker drop, complete control line adjustment etc.). This can simply be round a RIB. This way it is clear who was fastest to the mark, brings in some racing rules (who has room?) as well as practising a very important skill.

Downwind Riverboat

This is the reverse of the Upwind Riverboat, described on p33. There is a triangle with its base at the start / to windward and its apex at the leeward mark. Everyone has to stay in this triangle, which gets narrower the closer you get to the mark, requiring more frequent gybes.

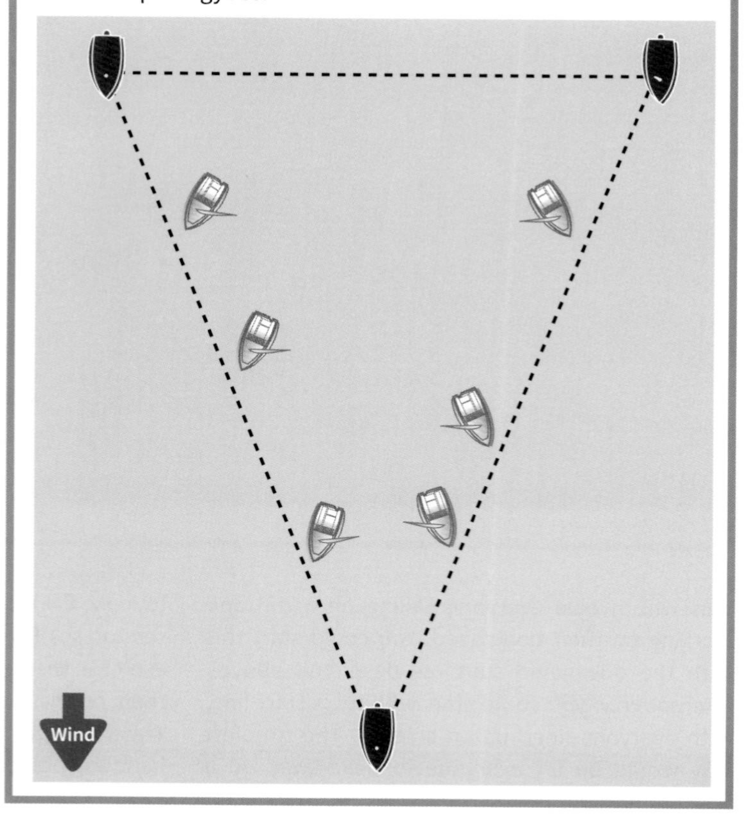

CHAPTER 10
Fitness

Active Recovery

Sailing is an endurance sport: we are not sprinters and most big competitions will take place over multiple races and multiple days, meaning that the way we recover is extremely important.

Rolling is probably one of the most effective ways of self-massage: you can target the specific area and repeatedly roll (think how you kneed bread to get out the lumps!). For small areas, a hard ball like a golf ball can work really well, although of course you can buy specialist equipment for various areas of the body such as spine massage.

Massage therapists can be of great help. Most professional teams will have one and they will often be able to get into areas that it is hard to target yourself. What is more they may be able to help suggest some exercises (tightness can often be caused by muscle imbalances or bad posture) or specific stretching to prevent the issue recurring.

Stretching increases flexibility. We can move around the boat better if we are flexible but also the stronger and more flexible muscles are, the less likely they are to be injured. We need to avoid muscle tears because, although the body does a wonderful job of repairing itself, you will never be quite the same as you were before the tear. Having a good range of motion will also help you in later life because, as we age, it becomes more difficult to maintain flexibility (think how flexible babies are!).

When starting or returning from a lengthy break, the process is the same: not to go too hard too early to avoid illness and injury because, in the long run, this means slower progress.

Diet

There are two elements to this: in simple terms fuel (supplying muscle glycogen to help you do the work the next day, normally best sourced through carbohydrates) and nutrition (the essential vitamins and minerals that your body needs).

Protein is used in repair, but not all protein sources are created equally. Clean foods (ones which are unprocessed) are a far better source than processed foods. For example, a pure chicken breast may contain 2g of fat per 100 grams, whereas a processed chicken slice may have 20 ingredients, most of which you really don't want added to your food.

Eating for health and fitness are not necessarily the same thing but they should be! Where possible, natural organic food should be preferable to taking vitamins and mineral supplements because often these man-made products have a poor availability (which means that not very much is absorbed).

Getting Ready For An Event

You may remember learning in school about the fire triangle: heat, fuel and oxygen. Remove one of the three key elements and the fire will go out. (If you cool the fire, remove the fuel or smother the oxygen, the fire will go out.)

It is the same in sailing. To develop your fitness there is a fitness triangle: good training, good sleep and good nutrition. If you remove one of these, while the 'fire' may not go out, you will find it very hard to make progress. In fact, if you end up with illness or injury, you may well go backwards.

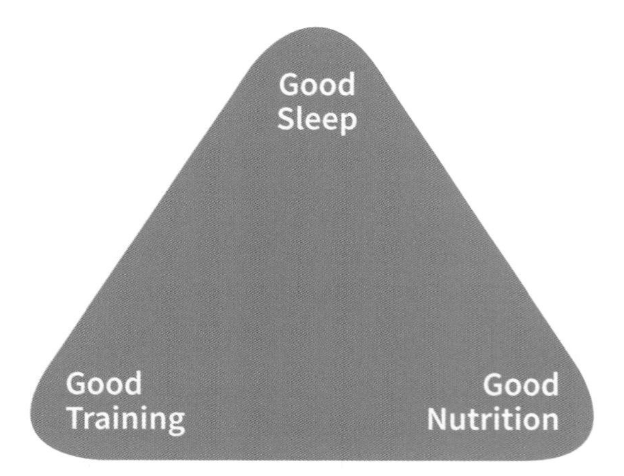

For a regatta you need a routine, and examples of this might be:

- 3-day taper where activity levels are gradually reduced, and carbohydrate loading occurs
- 1 complete rest day the day before (or more, for a very important / very windy regatta)
- A rest day, 2 days before; then a short session the day before, at a similar time and area of the race, to be focused

This is very much a personal thing: some people love the practice race; some people hate it. The point is to try different routines so that you know which works best for you and it becomes habit. You may then alter this as appropriate. So key performance regattas have a full taper and less important regattas just have 1 rest day in order to maximise the amount of sailing or other training you can do.

Exercise

This point is deliberately made last, as you need to think of the previous 2 points first. When you make a training plan, always put the rest days in first. Fatigue is part of training as, perhaps sometimes, is exhaustion. But, if you push yourself too hard and for too long, then illness and injury are likely to occur, and all the hard work training will be undone.

TOP TIP

A good warm-up not only prepares your body physically for training, it also improves your mental focus for sailing. This is why a good routine is so important, especially when doing explosive sessions. Being 'warm' (e.g. on a hot day) is not enough, the mind and body need to be prepared for exercise – they need to be warmed up.

The results of training are not always possible to see. The increased strength of core muscles which prevent injury for example, will not be as easy to see as the increased diameter of a bicep muscle, however the results (e.g. better speed in medium to strong winds) are!

Unfortunately, our minds do not always process negatives: we often only think about injuries when we are injured, aerobic fitness when we are too fatigued to sail well, or core strength when our back hurts.

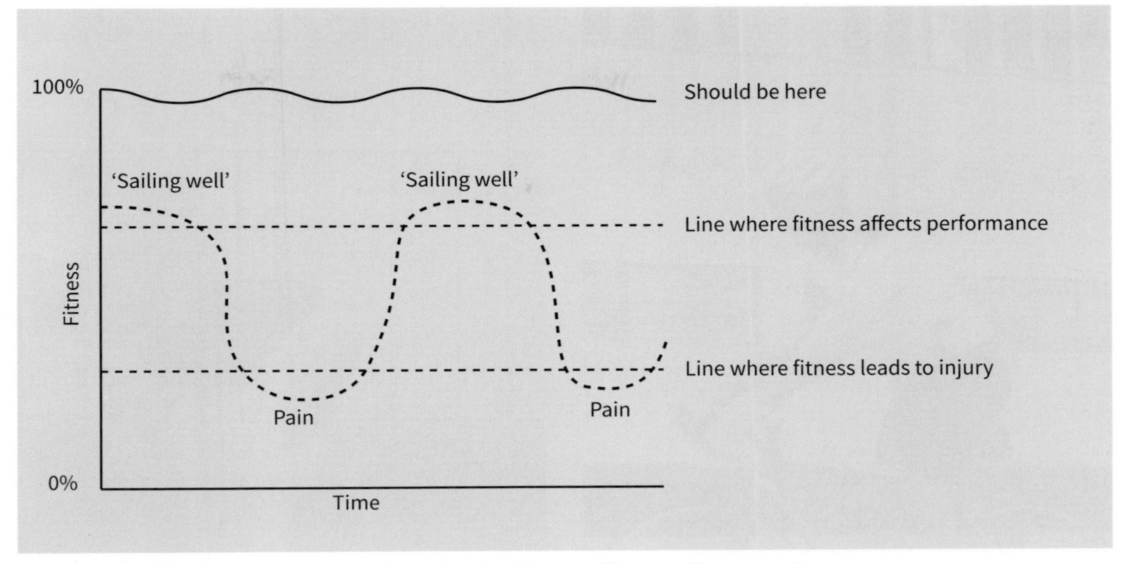

Fitness & injury lines – showing how different levels of fitness of fitness affect our sailing

We need to keep well above the line where our performance is limited by our fitness. We definitely need to be well above the line of pain because the longer and further below this line we go, the more likely injury is to occur. It then becomes a downward trend: the more time we spend in an injured state, the more likely it is to be permanent.

We want good training and good habits… so keep a training diary and put in rest days.

When planning your training, there are three key elements to consider:

1. Where in the programme is it best to do different sessions (periodisation)? For example:

- Work to increase stamina in the off season, so you can train longer when sailing more
- Work to increase strength / weight pre-season when it is easy to get to the gym and then become leaner and hit target weight for key regattas
- Reduce volume of training and do more explosive movements near your intended peak

2. When in your training day is it best to do different elements? For example:

- If fatigue is going to be an issue, always do your most technically demanding / important session first
- Allow sufficient breaks between sessions, maybe even having a nap: quality over quantity
- Consider how this session will affect subsequent sessions

3. What you are actually going to do? For example:

- Be specific: what goal are you trying to achieve (this may take 10-12 weeks plus and is part of your periodisation)
- Measure AND record the session to view progress and review and refine it
- By pushing one aspect of fitness (maximum heart rate, lift, time at aerobic threshold, stretch, core hold) you will, in the end, get greater return on that aspect than you would incorporating it in a general fitness programme. Push to fail and then the point of failure will be pushed back! You need to push the point of failure to move it. If you have a 30-horsepower engine and ask it to do 33-horsepower's work it will break; but the human body adapts. The point of failure moves and the 30-horsepower engine becomes a 33-horsepower engine and it can keep on improving…

One of the best ways of cardio-vascular fitness is cycling

After exercise, finish with stretches

Especially stretching your neck and back

END NOTE

It is hard to overestimate the importance of training. We have all heard the saying that the harder you train the luckier you get, but it is not that simple. It is not just about the effort put in but making that effort truly effective. This book combines over 20 years of coaching experience to ensure that everyone reading it has the opportunity to enjoy the most effective training possible.

I hope your training goes well.

COACH YOURSELF TO WIN

Jon Emmett

SAIL TO WIN

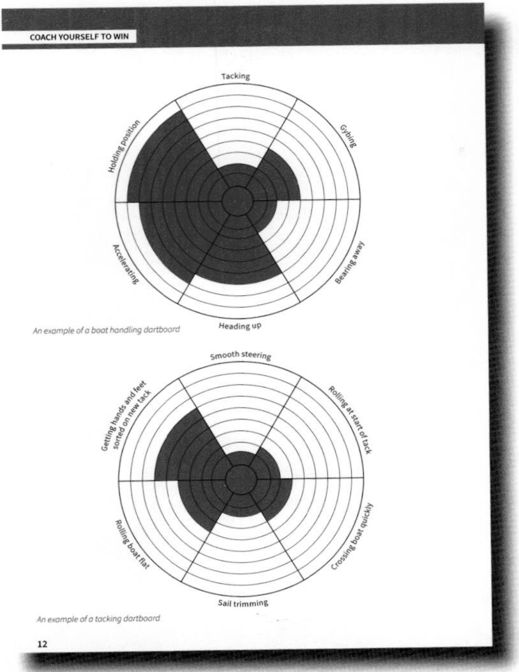

An example of a boat handling dartboard

An example of a tacking dartboard

sorted before rounding the mark and give yourself a wide enough entrance to the mark to ensure a tight exit. In a perfect world, if a picture were taken just one boat length after the mark, you should not be able to tell that you have just rounded it. So whenever training always finish on a good leeward mark rounding, as it is such an important skill.

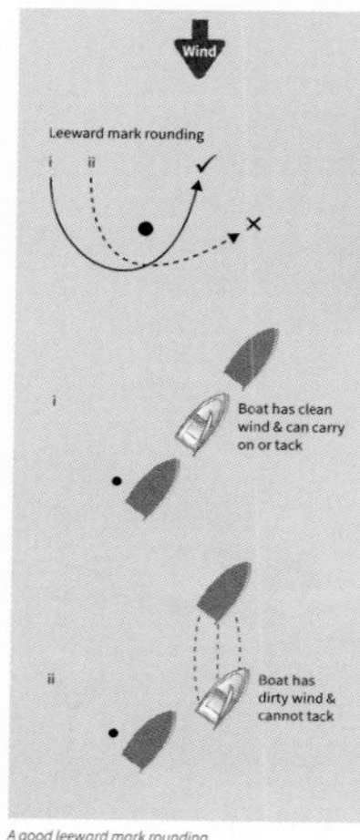

A good leeward mark rounding

Summary of Key Ideas

- Keep your wind clear or get into clean wind as soon as possible.
- Stay between the opposition and the next mark (directly upwind on the upwind legs, slightly offset on the downwind legs so as to have clean wind).
- Protect the favoured side of the course (the side with more wind, better current, etc.).

Advice from Olympic Gold Medallist (Laser class) Paul Goodison

“I feel the key to tactics is being able to adapt quickly to changing situations. It is very much about weighing up the risk / reward for each action on the race course. Try to minimise risk and sail conservatively. Generally, the people who make the fewest mistakes win.

It is important to be able to focus on the right thing at the right time. Different weather conditions and fleet positions will require different tactics. I try to keep things as simple as possible, and set myself small goals for different conditions. For example, in shifty conditions, I will always be on the lifted tack, sometimes even if this means that I am in dirty air. In stable conditions, I always make sure that I have clear wind. This may mean that I have to take a small header to clear my lane. I set out these goals for each day, as they are dependent on the conditions and stage of the regatta. It is easy to overcomplicate this area of sailing: generally the people that are winning are just keeping it simple.”

CHAPTER 2

Boat Handling

The phrase ‘boat handling’ refers to any skills that are not directly related to straight line speed. These can often be practised on land where the boat is securely tied to the trolley and you can analyse very carefully what is best to do with your hands and feet with no risk of a capsize.

The important thing is to be able to perform near perfect boat handling manoeuvres under pressure as this gives you lots of tactical options. For example, if you know that you can tack under someone without being rolled, or if you can gybe quickly making it hard for someone to cover you (or easier for you to cover them). You do so many tacks and gybes over the course of a race: if you can make each one just ⅓ boat length better, accumulatively that is a huge distance by the end of the race, and many fewer points at the end of a series.

It is also worth noting that slow speed boat handling skills, like those required pre-start, are very important too. It is not all about achieving rapid acceleration: being able to slow down, hold position and turn without going over a start line are all very important.

Practice

Practice makes perfect so, if you think of all the boat handling that you do during the course of a race, it is obvious that boat handling drills are an essential part of any campaign. When sailing high performance boats for the first time, just being able to get around the race course in the upper wind range can be a real achievement (and it is perhaps worth making sure that your first couple of sails are done in light to medium breezes!).

It is advisable to get your boat handling to a reasonable level before you hitch your boat up to go to your first open meeting as you cannot race effectively if your boat handling is not up to scratch (your strategy and tactics will be compromised if you cannot tack / gybe or get around the marks efficiently).

That old cliché: ‘time on the water’ is definitely true when it comes to perfecting boat handling, but remember that the more specific and demanding you make the exercises, the greater the potential improvement. By doing a good range of exercises (rather than simply going out and tacking and gybing) it is possible to keep motivation high, and old skills can soon be remembered again with intensive practice. In fact practising boat handling can be an excellent way of developing specific fitness (like doing fast spinnaker hoists and drops).

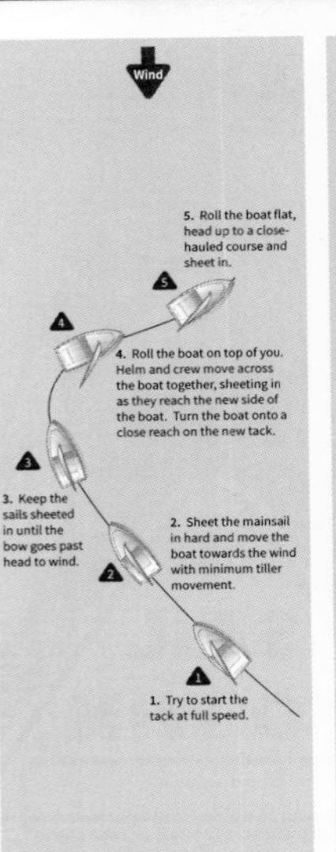

Best course to sail when tacking

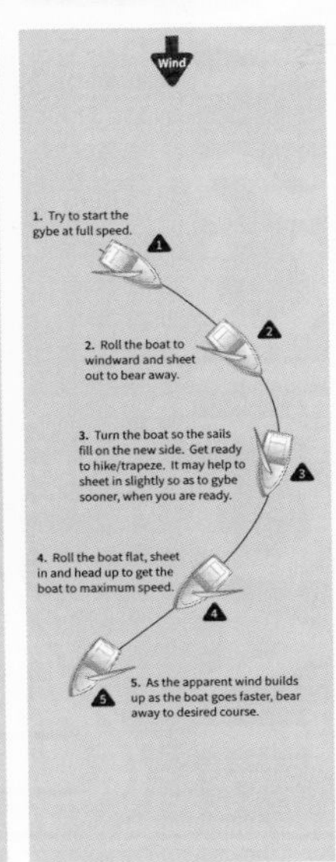

Best course to sail when gybing

TACTICS MADE SIMPLE

Jon Emmett

ANDREW SIMPSON FOUNDATION
THE SAILING CHARITY

SAIL
TO WIN

CHAPTER 3

Upwind

BASIC UPWIND SAILING (BEGINNER)

When you are sailing upwind your goal is to minimise the amount of time it takes you to get to the windward mark. It is not to maximise your speed (you could reach around all day and make no progress upwind), nor is it to point as close as possible to the wind (as you will end up going very slowly). Nevertheless, it is possible to sail a range of angles and still make equally good progress upwind (Velocity Made Good: VMG, that is speed in the desired direction) as demonstrated by Finlay Footing and Poppy Pinching.

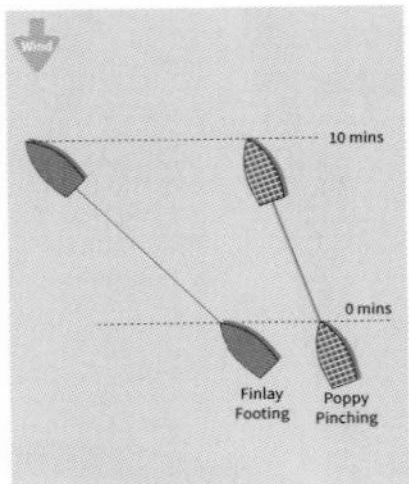

Finlay Footing and Poppy Pinching are sailing at different angles but have the same VMG because they travel the same distance upwind in the same time

However, in terms of ease of getting to the windward mark, somewhere in between is usually better as it is easier to sail to. The problem with Finlay Footing is that you can easily lose height for no extra speed (ending up sailing lower but the same speed) and the problem with Poppy Pinching is that you can easily lose speed trying to stay high. Being in the middle you are less likely to make an error as you can sail slightly higher or lower and still maintain maximum VMG. It will also probably be easier to hold your lane as this is likely to be the angle most other boats are sailing at.

But there are times when footing is very good: to get across to one side of the race course, perhaps to roll over another boat (get to windward and give them dirty air) or to get to a favoured side of the course: for example, out of bad current, into stronger wind or to be the first person into the new shift.

Likewise pinching has its place: if you want to stay away from one side of the course (it is a shifty day and you want to stay in the middle of the course) or perhaps to stay out of adverse tide or to leebow another boat.

So, for example, if you have been on starboard lift for a long time, you may tend to pinch on starboard tack so as not to get too far away from the centre of the course and then, as soon as the port lift comes in, foot on port tack to get back over to the centre of the course as quickly as possible.

This also means that you cross the other boats as soon as possible (you have not secured any gain to windward unless you are directly to windward of your rivals because, if the wind shifts again towards the other boats, they gain on you – so, if the wind went to the right, the boats on the right would gain.

If there is a slight lift as you tack, you may want to slow your tack down as otherwise you may come out slightly below the line you wanted to.

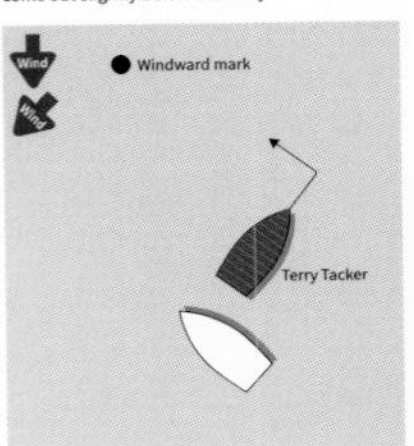

With a big wind shift, Terry is going to be over the layline, so tacks as soon as possible

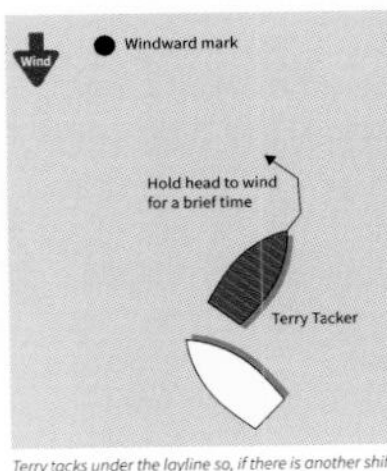

Terry tacks under the layline so, if there is another shift, he can take advantage of it

TACKING TO LOOSE COVER (INTERMEDIATE)

You may want to stay with a particular boat, for example, if the left-hand side of the beat is paying (you are making gains) or you expect it to gain. You don't want to completely separate from the boat or boats, but you stick to the side you expect to gain. This is when you apply a loose cover to stay with your rivals but not forcing them to tack by giving them dirty wind. This way they are likely to keep on going and you are in control.

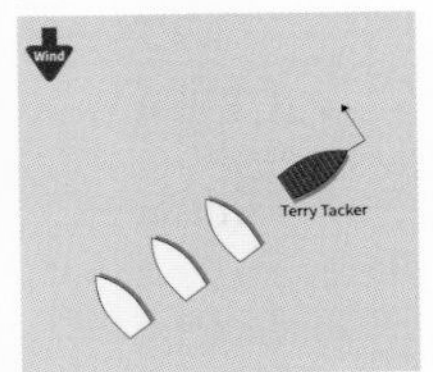

Terry tacks to give a loose cover, protecting the right

Terry tacks to give a loose cover, protecting the left

CHAPTER 7

Tight Reaching

TIGHT REACHING BASICS (BEGINNER)

One of the most important decisions to make is whether to hoist the kite and if so when! If you get it wrong and hoist too early, then you can make a big loss. Get it right and expect to make a significant gain on the fleet as there can be a large speed advantage to be flying the kite when other boats are not. For more details on rig set see chapter 5 in *Coach Yourself to Win*.

You must also consider current very carefully because, when your angle changes, so does the effect of the current. Once again, the danger is ending up too low for the mark. This may mean that you have to drop the kite to make it up and beat back up to the mark or, worse still, end up putting in a tack on a reach leg.

Many regattas will have a spacer mark before the downwind leg. This means you have a short tight reach to separate the fleet and avoid the carnage at the windward mark with boats going downwind meeting those who are still going upwind towards the windward mark. This is especially important for large fleets (perhaps sailing a sausage or inner loop) or very fast boats like twin trapeze catamarans. It is therefore important that the rig is set for a tight reach and then adjusted when you go round the spacer mark for the run. If there is a spacer mark, you should not set the rig for the run as soon as you round the windward mark.

DEALING WITH THE CONDITIONS (INTERMEDIATE)

Important information is what is the wind doing? Was it lifting at the windward mark? And if so, do you think it will continue to lift? Or is it now going to start to head? Are you expecting the wind to increase or decrease along the leg?

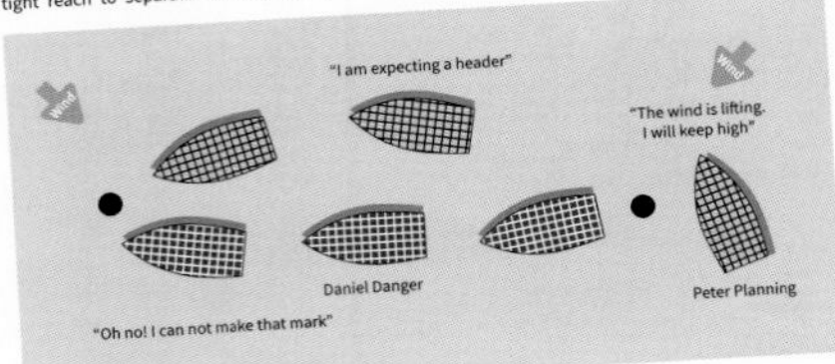

Peter Planning is expecting a wind shift

CHAPTER 16

The Final Beat

LONG FINAL BEAT (BEGINNER)

A long final beat (upwind finish) is rare nowadays although some classes still do this, or perhaps a race officer will choose to shorten the course at the windward mark on the final race of the day in fading light or wind (or indeed if the wind is becoming unmanageably too strong) with an offshore wind (as this gives the shortest sail home).

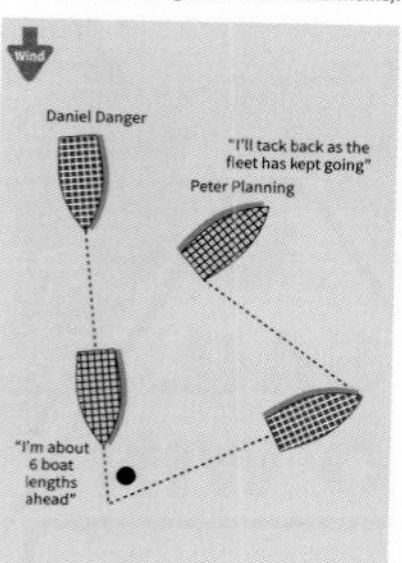

Peter Planning protects his position at the start of the last beat by tacking twice and applying a loose cover to keep between his rivals and the next mark

By the final beat, the fleet tends to be even more spread out, but this is no time to relax. Place changes can and do happen, and don't underestimate the psychological advantage of finishing a race with a massive lead!

The tactics involved in a long final beat are much the same as the second beat. Loose cover any boats you need to (unless you are consciously trying to sail another boat down the fleet). You should be concentrating on speed and getting across the finish line. Remember your 'position' is not safe until you cross that line and there are no guarantees in sailboat racing. Those boats miles in front of you could break something and you might still be able to overtake them before the finish.

If you are well clear of the boats behind and just want to defend your position, with no particular bias to the beat, then sail for approximately half the distance you are ahead, tack and sail for the other half. Then watch the boats behind. If they tack, go with them. If they don't tack, tack back to loose cover. This means you are not vulnerable to windshifts.

SHORT FINAL BEAT (INTERMEDIATE)

The short final beat usually becomes very much about the finish. You need to consider which end of the finish line and indeed which tack you are going to finish on before you round the leeward mark (see Chapter 17: The Finish).

It is often very hard to gain places, due to the short length of the leg. As there is not much time, it is difficult to get enough leverage. Instead you need to concentrate on not making unnecessary losses, for example, through doing lots of extra tacks or sitting in too much dirty wind.

HELMING TO WIN

Nick Craig

SAIL TO WIN

Where to Look when Racing

When you first start sailing, or are new to a boat, you tend to look at your feet to ensure that you aren't tripping up. The key to progressing is looking further and further up and knowing when to switch between the modes.

Broadly, there are 5 modes (places to look):

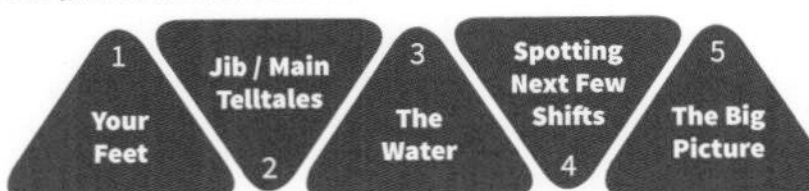

Mode 1: Your Feet

This is inevitable when you are new to the sport or a boat. It is an appropriate place to look when your boat handling is being pushed to its limit. Your boat handling limit will, of course, vary depending on how experienced you are in your chosen boat. However, you will miss a lot of windshifts and gusts if you look down too much.

You should move away from this mode as soon as possible, partly through being aware of where you are looking and by forcing yourself to look up. That can be hard as it may be outside your comfort zone and may mean that you fall over, or even out of the boat, occasionally, but it is a good thing to do at those training events.

Mode 2: Jib / Main Telltales

100% concentration on your telltales ensures that you are dead on the wind all of the time upwind and that your sails are always set optimally downwind. This is a good mode when boatspeed is critical, e.g. in a tight spot out of a start. However, you should eventually be able to keep your boat dead on the wind (or keep the sails optimally set) without spending much time staring at the telltales. Again, practice is key for this, forcing yourself to look at the water and not the jib is a good discipline.

Upwind Speed

The key reason why some people seem to be able to sail fast in any boat is good technique. Good technique means being able to sail a boat consistently flat and balanced as the wind changes in strength and direction with minimal use of the rudder. Often this is described as being 'in the groove'. Upwind speed is achieved by setting your boat up correctly and sailing it flat.

Getting 'In The Groove'

Sailing 'in the groove' is a wonderful feeling – you feel your boat sailing higher and faster than those around you.

Your boat is 'in the groove' when:

1. It is dead flat in all sea states.
2. Your foils are providing lift, as shown by slight weather helm (i.e. the boat tries to point to windward a touch when sailed flat).
3. Your sails are optimally set for the wind and wave conditions (which is a book in itself!).

Sailing Flat

Your boat needs to be sailed dead flat to be 'in the groove'. This is an unnatural position unless you have trained yourself to sail like this, because a few degrees of heel is more comfortable. An inclinometer (showing your angle of heel) is a useful training aid, and it is also helpful to look behind at the ripples from the rudder to see that they are even. Sailing consistently flat is much harder than sailing flat momentarily. To do it consistently you need to be anticipating the heeling effect of gusts and lulls which can only be achieved by having your head out of the boat.

In training, and in training events, a good objective is to sail flat all of the time. This may slow you up at first because you may be focusing on this rather than your telltales, the next gust or the multitude of other things that sailors can be looking for. But be persistent and eventually sailing flat will become a habit which you don't need to concentrate on. It is then a lifetime skill which will give you a permanent edge over most sailors. Sailing consistently flat is the biggest jump in speed most sailors can make, and the cheapest way to increase boatspeed!

Sailing flat, not even slightly heeled, is the biggest jump in speed most sailors can make

Lots of body steering is required to stay on the waves

Sailing at Championships

As I have already said, sailing is a very complex sport. At training events, you should try to keep dissecting the sport, experimenting with new ideas, learning, putting your processes back together and then breaking them up again.

At big events you should keep it simple. Stop trying new things and sail instinctively. Most big events are won or lost before the event, so what you have learnt through the season will now show through. It is too late to change anything now, so this is the time to enjoy putting everything together and sail at your best without the distraction of training objectives!

By trying new things at the smaller events, the big events are in many ways easier, which is a nice mindset with which to go into a championship.

The best practice to get good at big fleet sailing is, unsurprisingly, big fleet sailing! Experienced big fleet sailors are able to glance around quickly and understand immediately where they are versus the fleet, understand how much risk they are taking and assess that against their objectives. This sounds complex but with experience it becomes almost instinctive, so the sailor is focused on speed rather than having to look around at the fleet too much.

While a little tedious, checklists can be useful at big events as it is easy to forget something critical (e.g. food, the most important thing!). A checklist should include all the things you need, e.g. multitool, tape, spares, food, water, etc.

Being able to start well in big fleets is a key skill

CREWING TO WIN
Saskia Clark
ANDREW SIMPSON FOUNDATION
THE SAILING CHARITY
SAIL
TO WIN

Flying the spinnaker in light winds

The lighter the wind becomes the harder it is to trim: drop the pole height which will give the spinnaker a bit of weight again and make it easier to fly. As soon as the wind builds, raise the pole height again to give your spinnaker depth and power.

Flying the spinnaker with the guy not in the cleat

As you improve you might uncleat the guy rope and keep the tension in your arm for quick and easy trimming. Although this is good for accurate guy position beware of losing any power through your arm as a gust comes on. If it's cleated the gust can transfer power straight into the spinnaker.

Heavy Wind Trimming

This is the opposite to light wind trim: the windier it becomes the more you want to strap the spinnaker close to the boat so it doesn't roll around and take charge of the steering. Tightening both sheet and guy towards the boat stretches the spinnaker out and flattens the shape so it is less powerful.

Boat Heel And Trim

There will be constant little adjustments to make in your body weight with all the fluctuations in wind. As general rule, in the lighter stuff you'll be sat right next to the shroud with your legs positioned so that you can move your weight inboard easily if

CHAPTER 3

A Day On The Water

What To Wear

If you are just giving sailing a go then just wear something that you are happy to get wet in, ideally quick drying and take some kind of wind / waterproof jacket if you have it, as it will always be colder on the water than you are expecting. Any kind of trainers will be fine.

If you are committed to spending some money, then my vote would be for a good fitting wetsuit with quality neoprene, so it is nice and flexible. I prefer wearing a long john wetsuit and layering up on thermals as it gets cold, rather than a steamer, to keep mobility in my shoulders and elbows.

Boots with a good grip but flexible sole are a vital bit of crewing equipment. Some people pull off bare feet whilst crewing, but stubbing your toe is one of the most painful experiences known to humans, so it's not something for me. Also, there is the uncomfortable bit of launching in bare feet.

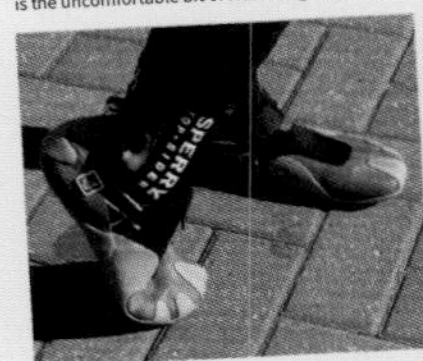

My boots are flexible, but with good grip

For me, gloves are a must when going out sailing, except if it is very light winds. I use full-finger gloves except for thumb and index finger, so that you can do fiddly knots and split rings. It's important that the gloves are not so thick that you lose grip.

I use full-finger gloves except for the thumb and index finger

In the summer, many like to wear a baseball hat to keep the sun and spray out their eyes. In the winter, a woolly hat is an affordable way to stay comfortable in cold weather. Do ensure there is somewhere to put it during a race if things heat up. This can be a pouch on the boat somewhere or it can just be tucked under a buoyancy aid.

Starting Drills

An output of your strategy discussion should be a decision on where you want to start, and it should be a start that complements your upwind strategy but not one that would make it impossible.

If you've decided that holding out to the left of the course is vital, then a pin end start is the most preferable option. However, the pin end can often be a highly congested area, so you might consider starting in space further up the line, lessening the risk of starting in a congested area, executing a reasonable start to hold your lane and not get immediately bounced to the right. There will, of course, be races when the outcome is decided at the start and you have to be the boat that executes the start in a congested area in order to win, but this probably happens on fewer occasions than people think, and, in a series of races, it become less vital to be that boat.

Whatever your starting decision, it is worth doing a few warm up starts, especially when there is tide. Evaluate where you want to start, figure out where the layline is for that position, how much drift there is when you are downspeed and flapping, what the slowest speed is that you need to be moving for the amount of wind to keep grip on the foils; and do a few practice accelerations so you know how long it takes you to get from stationary to full speed.

Practise starts: from a slow speed

Bear away to build up speed

Lean the boat to leeward to help luff up and get speed

To power over the line at full speed

CHAPTER 5

Trapezing Technique

When starting out trapezing remember that pretty much the worst that can happen is that you get wet.

The worst thing that can happen when trapezing is that you get wet

Any anxiety you have about trapezing will quickly go, so let's get started and out on the wire!

- Trim your jib to the correct place.
- Pull your hook height so you will just skim the deck when attached and have the jibsheet in your back hand.
- Clip on and relax in your harness and feel that the trapeze wire is taking your weight.
- As the wind increases, and the boat begins to tip, use your back leg on the floor / centreboard case to push yourself out over the side until your front leg finds it's footing on the gunwale. Use your hands to steady yourself on the gunwale or shroud if needed.
- As the wind further increases, straighten your front leg until your back foot can join your front foot on the gunwale.
- If you've lost your jibsheet in the process crouch down and get it or get your helm to pass it out to you.

THE ANDREW SIMPSON SAILING FOUNDATION

The charity was founded to honour the life and legacy of Andrew 'Bart' Simpson MBE, Olympic Gold & Silver medalist and America's Cup Sailor by using sailing to improve the lives of young people.

Working with sailing providers internationally, the Foundation offers the challenges of a sailing environment to promote health and wellbeing, and to develop personal skills that will improve a young person's ability to succeed in life.

SUPPORT US

info@andrewsimpsonsailing.org
andrewsimpsonfoundation.org

@AndrewSimpsonSa Andrew Simpson Sailing Foundation
andrewsimpsonsailingfoundation # sailonbart